FOX
TOSSING

>>>———→

AND OTHER FORGOTTEN
AND DANGEROUS
SPORTS, PASTIMES, AND GAMES

←———<<<

EDWARD
BROOKE-HITCHING

A TOUCHSTONE BOOK

NEW YORK   LONDON   TORONTO   SYDNEY   NEW DELHI

Touchstone
An Imprint of Simon & Schuster, Inc.
1230 Avenue of the Americas
New York, NY 10020

Copyright © 2015 by Edward Brooke-Hitching

Originally published in 2015 in Great Britain by Simon & Schuster UK Ltd.

First Touchstone hardcover edition November 2015

TOUCHSTONE and colophon are registered
trademarks of Simon & Schuster, Inc.

For information about special discounts for bulk purchases,
please contact Simon & Schuster Special Sales at
1-800-456-6798 or business@simonandschuster.com.

Interior design by Jill Putorti

Manufactured in the United States of America

10 9 8 7 6 5 4 3 2 1

Library of Congress Cataloging-in-Publication Data is available.

ISBN 978-1-5011-1514-1
ISBN 978-1-5011-1517-2 (ebook)

For my parents
(the best sports of all)

CONTENTS

CONTENTS

INTRODUCTION

Sport; something that unbends the mind by turning it off from care.
Samuel Johnson

On January 21, 2014, the head of the largest golf equipment company in the world told a conference of American industry professionals that their sport was dying. Addressing the recent dramatic fall in player numbers, Mark E. King, then CEO of TaylorMade, convened the meeting at Florida's Rosen Centre to appeal for suggestions as to how to rescue their game from mortal peril.

"We've lost five million over the last ten years!" cried one speaker, Joe Beditz, CEO of the National Golf Foundation, as he stood backed by a giant projection that screamed "5,000,000 LOST." "Five million! And that's out of thirty million!" Figures showed that—in the United States at least—the core group of golfers, defined as those who play at least eight rounds a year, had decreased in number by about 25 percent.

"One out of four!" said Beditz. "And those core golfers are responsible for ninety percent of spending and rounds played in golf . . ."

Whether golf is destined to go the way of the dodo is yet to be seen, but the salient point suggested by the TaylorMade panic is this: a sport's immortality is not guaranteed. And if it can die, it can be forgotten.

The idea for this book was inspired by Hans Friedrich von Fleming's *Der vollkommene teutsche Jäger*, or *The Perfect German Hunt*, published in 1719. My eye was caught by a particularly puzzling image, depicting an entertainment called *Fuchsprellen*. Although my eighteenth-century German is frankly a little *rostig*, the unusual combination of the words for "fox" and "bouncing" was unmistakable. This conclusion was helped by the artwork itself, which shows well-dressed nobles casually slinging the splay-legged creatures heavenward. I sent my notes to an antiquarian book dealer, asking if he had ever come across the sport before. His response was that if I wished to hoax him successfully, I had better come up with something more plausible.

Here is a sport that seems to have slipped through the net of mainstream historical record, and yet is one of the most fascinatingly eccentric aspects of Teutonic hunting history (which, let me tell you, is really saying something). The fact that *Fuchsprellen* has maintained such a low profile over the years begged the question: how many other sports like this have been forgotten? *Fox-tossing and Other Forgotten . . . Games* examines hidden pockets of history to find the answers.

The word "sport" comes from the Old French word "*desporter*," meaning "to divert, amuse, take pleasure." Before the relatively recent concept of establishing a rule book, this idea of a sport being any particular active pastime indulged in for pleasure (especially hunting) is how it was thought of for centuries. For example, Samuel Johnson's principal definition of the word in his dictionary of 1755 is: "Play; diversion; game; frolick and tumultuous merriment," with an alternative entry declaring it "Diversion of the field, as of fowling, hunting, fishing." This book draws on both old and modern criteria to welcome the peripheral and ephemeral alongside the traditional, in an effort to comprehensively chart the various forgotten forms that sport has taken throughout history.

For, until recently, writers and historians haven't considered sport to be particularly worthy of record, and we are left with fewer details of it than of other aspects of period life. Yet from learning about how our ancestors entertained themselves we gain a unique insight into broader contemporary attitudes toward morality, humor, and the trials of daily existence. In fact, sport has frequently played a significant role in the development of civilization. For the Romans, the games in the Colosseum and other giant arenas were often as much political demonstrations of superior might as they were entertainment for the rabble; in England efforts were frequently made by authorities to ban early forms of sports such as soccer for fear they were distracting people from the practice of those activities with martial applications, such as archery and swordplay. Edward III was a particular opponent. His reign had seen the devastation of the Black Death, and as a result his army was in desperate need of well-trained recruits to recharge the depleted ranks. A decree issued in 1363 commanded the English citizenry to abandon frivolous pursuits:

> We ordain that you prohibit under penalty of imprisonment all and sundry from such stone, wood, and iron throwing; handball, football, or hockey; coursing and cockfighting, or other such idle games.

Sport also has a long history of causing clashes with the Church, and laws intended to preserve the Sabbath were often flouted in favor of kicking an inflated pig's bladder around, as well as games such as quoits and just about anything that could be gambled on. The situation was no doubt exacerbated by the fact that in the early form of soccer, which consisted of teams of entire villages playing against each other, in order to score a goal one was required to kick the ball into the opposing village's churchyard. It was also an incredibly violent activity in which damage to property, injuries, and even deaths were commonplace. The Puritan writer Philip Stubbes railed against the violence of ball games in his *The Anatomie of Abuses* (1583):

> Sometimes their necks are broken, sometimes their backs, sometimes their legs, sometimes their arms, sometimes one part is thrust out of joint, sometimes the noses gush out with blood . . . Football encourages envy and hatred . . . sometimes fighting, murder and a great loss of blood.

Little changes.

Despite the fact that the more peripheral sports were often overlooked by those documenting contemporary affairs, the information is available to those willing to dig. The entries presented here are drawn from wildly varying sources: from Suetonius to Shakespeare; from the Icelandic sagas to fourteenth-century Florentine manuscripts; from the *Kentish Gazette* of 1794 to Lord Baden-Powell's seminal 1889 encomium *Pig-sticking or Hoghunting*. In studying these forgotten games, many unexpected and fascinating discoveries are made, such as the extent to which London theater owes its origins to the vicious animal-baiting pits; the bloody coining of the phrase "to beat around the bush"; and even the ancient history of the spiked dog collar (as it turns out, it has a practical application aside from causing your parents to worry over your lifestyle choices).

The reasons why these forgotten sports fell out of favor are, of course, many and varied, but broadly speaking can be divided into three categories: cruelty, danger, and ridiculousness. "Cruelty" covers the widest area here. As a species we are aware of our (continuing) terrible track record covering treatment of animals, but it isn't until one delves into the history of animal-baiting that the true extent is realized, in all its bizarre forms. Sports such as eel-pulling, pig-sticking, the whimsical Italian cat head butting, and, of course, fox tossing all fall under this purview: these "games" are senselessly brutal, but to players of the era they were merely light pre-supper entertainment. As society developed and it began to be frowned upon to treat animals as projectiles, these entertainments were outlawed and left to rot in history's undercroft.

Under "danger" one can gather the group of sports that dwindled, or only briefly existed, thanks to the enormous amount of personal risk involved. Worthy of mention here are sports such as balloon jumping, waterfall-riding, and firework boxing, all representing different eras and yet all requiring of their participants that common characteristic of total insanity. Initially, of course, the element of danger formed the basis of their daredevil appeal, but whenever something carries with it a high "frequent death" quotient, it usually becomes old news fast. Such was the case here, through either legislation or a rediscovered desire to live.

Finally, "ridiculousness" is best exemplified by the sport of ski ballet, in which a lycra-clad Frankenstein's monster was created by stitching together stunt skiing, ice dancing, and terrible fashion sense. Inevitably when researching a book such as this one develops favorites, and I must confess that, out of all the sports deserving of resurrection, I live in hope that someday it will again be possible to witness a Ski Ballet Championship.

Every sport needs its personalities, champions, and pioneers: for balloon jumping this was Aircraftman "Brainy" Dobbs; for fox tossing it was King Augustus the Strong; for ski ballet it was Suzy "ChapStick" Chaffee. A personal hero, though, is John Joseph Merlin, the inventor of the roller skate. The eccentric Belgian engineer was responsible for a variety of intricate inventions, musical instruments, and automata (including the stunning Silver Swan currently housed in the Bowes Museum), but it was the disastrous debut of his wheeled shoe in 1760 that made his name. The writer Joseph Strutt recounts the events of the grand unveiling (*Sports and Pastimes*, 1801). Bear in mind as you read the following that, according to other sources, Monsieur Merlin was simultaneously playing the violin at the time:

> Joseph Merlin of Liege, who came to England with the Spanish ambassador in 1760, invented a pair of skates that ran on wheels. But his exhibition of them was not a success. Gliding about in them at a masquerade at Carlisle House, Soho Square, he ran into a valuable mirror worth £500, which he completely shattered in addition to wounding himself severely.

INTRODUCTION

The idea for this book started with an image of eighteenth-century Germans catapulting foxes into the air for fun, and the strangeness developed from there; eccentricity is not just included but celebrated. Provided here is a collection of windows into periods of history so startling that they push the limits of credibility and invoke a new level of appreciation for the humor, the ingenuity, and, at times, the sheer madness of our ancestors.

AERIAL GOLF

Golf courses can be hazardous places—stray balls, lightning, the occasional alligator—and for golfers in the 1920s, there was even a period when you were at serious risk of being dive-bombed by light aircraft.

"Aerial golf" made its first official appearance on May 27, 1928, at the Old Westbury Golf Club on Long Island. The teams were made up of one player on the course and one pilot in the skies above, who would "tee off" by dropping balls from his aircraft onto the green, to then be holed by his teammate. In this instance, the pilots were Arthur Caperton and M. M. Merrill, who took off from Curtiss Airfield in planes loaded with sackfuls of gutta-percha golf balls. Once over the course, the men swooped fifty feet above the ground and delivered their payload, tossing a ball over the side as near to the hole as possible on each of the nine greens. Spectators crowded the course as the match unfolded, and, it was reported, some even observed from light aircraft of their own.

As it turned out, Merrill was a natural aerial golfer. Each of his "drives" landed neatly near the target, making it easy for his partner on the ground, William Hammond, to sink the putt. Caperton, however, was slightly wilder with his aim, and his unfortunate teammate, William Winston, was forced to hack three balls out of the rough. In the end, Merrill/Hammond defeated Caperton/Winston 3 up. Two months later another match was organized, this time featuring the participation of US Congressman Fiorello

La Guardia, and by 1931 even the great baseball star Ty Cobb could be seen in the skies over Georgia, hurling golf balls from the passenger seat of an American Eagle monoplane.

Interestingly, there was also an unrelated sport played earlier called "airplane golf," which was a completely different game. A match was played in Texas in 1918 featuring an "aerial golf field" 180 miles across—the "holes" were postboxes hammered into the soil of nine separate meadows. The competitors took off from Call Field and, using only compass bearings, had to locate each "green." They were then to land, write their name and the time of their arrival on a piece of paper, slip it into the postbox, and take to the skies again to find the next hole. In Britain, a variation also emerged in which male and female aviators dropped flour bombs onto targets below, obliterating manicured English greens in explosions of white powder. These competitions were played around the world in various forms (sometimes with small parachutes attached to the balls) until the outbreak of World War II, when priorities shifted somewhat.

THE AQUATIC TRIPOD

When it came to hunting waterfowl, the drawback for some was having to remain on dry land, watching helplessly as your prey paddled away. The development of punt gunning (covered later) was certainly one solution to this hindrance, but that sport was less about pursuit and more about obliteration.

An alternative idea appeared in the 1820s. The aquatic tripod was the device of choice for the determined fowler, and must have been a hell of a thing to see in action. The machine was composed of three curved iron rods joined in the middle to support a seat for the hunter. At the other end of each rod was soldered a circular iron pontoon, made of two discs the size of large dinner plates welded together. The hunter perched on the saddle that doubled as a chest support, allowing him to lean into his shot. Stirrups were also provided for extra security. For those with a bigger duck-blasting budget, optional extras were available, such as a fixture for a fishing rod, another for the gun, and a handy basket in which to deposit the bagged game.

All of this would, of course, be useless without the means to propel the framework across the water. A Scotsman named Mr. Kent is credited with the solution: two five-inch paddles made from block tin that could be attached by leather straps to the soles of the rider's boots. With these, a leisurely walking speed could be achieved by employing an action similar to that of an ice skater. When sudden acceleration was called for, the rider grabbed

The aquatic tripod. Illustration from
John Badcock's *Domestic Amusements* (1823)

hold of his chest support and kicked out with both legs simultaneously like a frogman.

The aquatic tripod first came into use in England in the winter of 1822, when the countryside was rich with migratory Arctic birds. The *Chester Chronicle* wrote at the time:

> These birds have had a desperate and fatal enemy in two men, from (we believe) Lincolnshire; they have a sort of raft, on which they float along the margins of rivers or lakes left by the tide. On this raft is a large gun, etc. Without further information, however, than just quoted . . . we strongly suspect that the sort of raft spoken of is no other than the Aquatic Tripod, or Tricipede, which has been lately used on some waters of Lincolnshire, with complete success.

It wasn't just among the inland waterways and lakes of Britain that the tripod could be found, however. In *Domestic Amusements* (1823), John Badcock mentions a gentleman named Andrew Scheerborn, of Scheveningen, Holland, who built his own model, said to be more remarkable for strength than ingenuity. The Dutchman frequently took his machine out on to the open waters of the North Sea, somehow managing to survive terrible waves that broke twelve feet high.

AUTO POLO

The noble sport of horseback polo, known as "the game of kings," has a rich history dating all the way back to the sixth century BC, when it was devised as a training exercise for cavalry troops in Persia. From there the game spread far and wide, to Egypt and China, Japan and Constantinople, and India, where it caught the eye of the British. For nearly two thousand years the sport existed in its original form, until one day everything changed, as is so often the way, when an American got his hands on it. Enter "auto polo."

"If you don't die of fright, you'll laugh yourself to death," a fan told the *Miami News* in 1924. "I have seen every known variety of sport in the world, but auto polo has them all beat for action and speed. If you have a weak heart and cannot stand excitement, auto polo is a good game to stay away from."

The idea to replace the agile thoroughbred polo pony with a spluttering motor car can be traced to back to 1902, when one of the earliest known auto polo matches took place in Boston. A member of the elite Dedham Polo Club named Joshua Crane Jr. announced an exhibition of a new game. Crane was an accomplished polo player and automobile driver, and it hadn't taken him long to combine his two passions. Before a crowd at the Dedham grounds he drove out onto the field, and to their bemusement began swinging at balls with a mallet while steering with the other hand. "The play is executed so quickly that an unpracticed eye has difficulty in following it," wrote the *Chicago Daily Tribune* of the Crane game. "The nimble little mobile machines used in the game are capable of developing a speed of about forty miles an hour in a few feet and can be brought to a standstill practically within their own lengths."

The introduction of the automobile into daily life had brought with it the thrill of high speed, and for the new generation of adrenaline junkies, polo ponies were suddenly a rather tame option. When the Model T was brought out in 1908, it instantly became the car favored by auto polo enthusiasts thanks to its affordability, light weight, and sturdy resistance to frequent tumbling.

As the game developed the rules were refined, but were in essence similar to those of horseback polo. The field was usually about 300 feet long by 120 wide, with two goal areas marked by stakes driven into the ground 15 feet apart at each end. The aim of the game was to dribble the ball—similar in size to a basketball—past your four-wheeled opponent and wallop it home. The referee, meanwhile, had to ensure fair play while dodging the zooming vehicles on foot, frequently calling "time" to allow collided vehicles to disentangle themselves, or for the mallet-man to retake his seat, having leapt from the moving car to escape an imminent crash. The players had this maneuver down to a fine art and would swiftly resume, once it was established that no medical attention was required. Seat straps were soon installed to reduce unwanted ejections, and an early form of a roll cage was fitted to the car's frame to reduce unwanted crushings. The cars frequently turned over completely, and, in the event they were left upside down, it was up to the players to extract themselves and right their own vehicle.

In fact, in its more aggressive moments the sports had as much in common with the rough-and-tumble of a modern demolition derby than it did with horseback polo. To the thrill of the crowd, drivers would often initially ignore the ball and ram their opponents to flip them over, turning their attention to scoring goals only once the other contestants were incapacitated. This, of course, made it terrific fun to watch. Its popularity also came from the fact that it could be played under cover, unlike horseback polo, which demanded a huge amount of space to accommodate eight ponies galloping around. With auto polo, the vehicles could brake more sharply and turn on a dime. This meant there were many more venues suitable for hosting a game, making it a comfortable, perennial spectator sport when played under shelter.

Auto polo enjoyed broad news coverage, and its popularity spread across America. Clubs were formed, and proponents performed demonstration matches at fairs, sporting events, and circuses. The inherent danger of being tossed, crushed, and walloped was just as exciting for the crowd to watch as it was for the players to undergo ("It would be hard to devise a game in which the players took bigger chances of mishap," wrote a journalist in

An auto polo contest in Regina, Saskatchewan, in 1919 shows just how dangerous the sport was. (*Glenbow Museum Archives NC-38-4*)

1912), and lent proceedings a uniquely exhilarating atmosphere, to which the *Prescott Journal Miner* of November 7, 1917, attests:

> If one comes to these games expecting to be mildly amused, they will receive, to their intense satisfaction, the biggest surprise in the world. You will laugh, you will hold your breath, and the chills will creep up your spine. The very air at an auto polo contest seems to be surcharged with excitement, while waves of sympathetic feeling and enthusiasm push from one end of the grandstand to the other.

The sport even found fans among royalty. In 1913 a team of auto polo players from Wichita, Kansas, traveled to England to perform a demonstration for King George V, who was keen to see the how the game of kings had been improved by the Americans. The sport was met with such adulation that the players embarked on a two-week tour of Europe. By the 1930s, however, enthusiasm for the sport had waned, perhaps due to the fact that frequent damage and injury brought a high financial cost, but also because the novelty of the sight had worn off; public interest had roamed elsewhere, to newer excitements such as auto rodeo, in which cowboys lassoed and rounded up steers from motor cars.

BABY BOXING

Spike Webb was a respected boxer and former US Army sergeant who in 1919 became an associate professor and boxing coach at the United States Naval Academy in Annapolis, Mary-

A baby boxing match from January 21, 1933.
Two of the youngest kid boxers at the Academy are shown sparring.
Gordon Baird White (left) was the three-year-old son of Lieutenant and
Mrs. T. B. White, and Toddy Carroll (four years old) was the son
of Lieutenant and Mrs. Chester E. Carroll. (*NEA*)

land. "He taught guts to the midshipmen," said Admiral Robert B. Pirie. "The things learned from him enabled us to stick it out when the going got rough." Admiral William F. Halsey Jr. once declared: "Spike Webb is the greatest psychologist I have ever known in my life."

Webb's first act on arriving at the academy was to establish the Navy Junior Boxing Program, which was a training course in full-contact boxing designed to toughen up the young sons of both officers and civilians serving there. The program was open to boys aged between five and eleven years, who would undergo weeks of training before competing in the Navy Junior Boxing Finals. The sport was quickly nicknamed "baby boxing" by journalists who filmed the annual event for international newsreels.

The boys were matched with opponents of equal size, and, after donning miniature gloves, fought several rounds of full-contact boxing in front of an audience of classmates and parents. Matches were considerably shorter than those fought by adult combatants, and the baby boxers, who on average weighed in at about fifty pounds, were more easily forgiven for becoming disheartened by a blow to the nose and seeking out the arms of their mother in the crowd.

In 1962 Tony Rubino took over the program, and around 126 boxers, weighing between 30 and 110 pounds, trained for five weeks before competing in the finals that year. The following is a letter Rubino sent to the boxers of the forty-third annual program:

To the Boys of the Navy Junior Boxing Class,

Dear Boys:

The Navy Junior Boxing Program, of which you are now a part, offers you many chances to become a better young man. In boxing, the spirit of "give and take" is part of the game. Life has always demanded the courage to "take it" and the ability to come back fighting. You will learn in this program that you can face a setback, and then return to the battle unafraid.

You will learn how to use your body and your mind together. You will learn much about confidence and calmness while under pres-

sure. All-important, boys, is the fact that you are learning to play fair. If you learn this well, you will never think of being a bully.

Boys who learn to box become strong in spirit as well as in body. You will learn good sportsmanship. You will learn, boys, that true glory is not in winning, but in trying. You will carry honor away with you this afternoon when you leave MacDonough Hall. You are all champions. For to be a champion, one must always do his best.

Navy Juniors, it is a real pleasure to have you on the youngest team in the entire Navy. Your parents, I am sure, join me in passing on to you a much deserved "well done."

At the conclusion of the Finals youngsters will be awarded the Navy "N," the Navy medal, and a copy of the official program, after which gallons of ice cream, milk, and cookies will be served by the mothers.

The Navy Junior Boxing Finals continued to be held annually into the late 1970s.

BALLOON JUMPING

It is the 1920s, and you are standing in an open field. There are no sounds, other than the rustle of buffeted leaves and the faint notes of lark song. The summer sun warms your face. As the breeze brushes past, you break into a run and launch yourself into the sky. You're flying through the air, impossibly, yet possible because the enormous helium-filled balloon to which you're har-

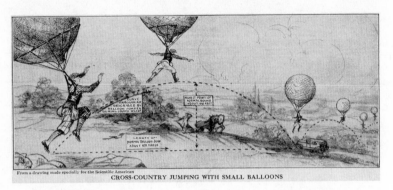

From a drawing made specially for the Scientific American
CROSS-COUNTRY JUMPING WITH SMALL BALLOONS

A 1927 edition of *Scientific American* paints an idyllic impression
of how cross-country balloon jumping might work.

nessed is dragging you with it as it soars hundreds of feet. Farms, forests, and meadows are stretched out below as you float over the landscape, legs dangling high above baffled farmers and terrified cows. Gradually you tail into a gentle descent, landing lightly on your feet. You scan your surroundings for where to go next as the balloon tugs on the ropes. You decide the sycamores to the west look like sport and bound toward them like a lunar explorer, leaping up to a branch before springing from bough to bough and sailing right over a tree. You feel like Peter Pan. Suddenly, the world is small and life is limitless . . .

It should have been revolutionary. "How would you like to own your own hand-power jitney balloon," cried *Popular Science* in its April 1923 edition, "to spend your Saturday afternoons joy-riding in the sky, up a thousand feet or so, swinging beneath the round belly of a small gas-filled bag and traveling anywhere you can induce the playful breezes to take you?"

The "jumping balloon" or "hopper balloon" was the invention of M. Q. Corbett, W. E. Hoffman, and C. F. Adams of the "lighter than air" division of the US Army based at McCook Field, Ohio. Consisting of a giant air bag attached by ropes to a wooden bench, the devices were initially used by maintenance workers as cheap tools for inspecting the outer surfaces of large airships and hot air balloons and carrying out repairs.*

As their use spread, people began to imagine how the personal balloons could be used for fun. The claim that only minimal training was required to operate them caused particular excitement, prompting visions of businessmen balloon-jumping their way to work and schoolboys raining from the sky.

"How helpful this sort of thing would be," said the July 19, 1927, edition of Missouri's *Joplin News Herald*, envisioning the sport as an aid for climbers and the elderly. "We could strip the spring cherry tree without endangering our legs. We could dispense with elevators and enter our offices on the third or fourth floors by merely leaping up to the window and crawling in. We could do a thousand and one things easily that we now do with difficulty."

The perceived ease of use was down to the simplicity of the controls: altitude was gained simply by leaping into a mild to mid-strength wind; and, unlike hot air balloons, there was no need to shed ballast or vent gas, because it was carefully ensured

---

* They were also useful for emergency deployment: when the stratospheric balloonist Georgy Prokofiev attempted a second launch of the doomed *USSR-3* project on March 16, 1939, the giant aircraft failed to escape its safety net, and two men in hopper balloons were sent to free it from the tangled mess. While doing so, one of the would-be rescuers lost his balance and fell from his vehicle, catching hold of a rope dangling from *USSR-3* to save himself. Despite the heroic efforts of the hopper balloonists, disaster struck as the *USSR-3* reached an altitude of 1,200 meters. A valve was torn open, and the gigantic gas bag crashed in the woods halfway between Kuntsevo and central Moscow.

that the weight of the balloonist slightly exceeded the pull of the balloon—thus the chances of disappearing into the stratosphere were minimized. The bag itself was roughly eighteen feet in diameter and capable of holding three thousand cubic feet of hydrogen or helium gas. The latter was preferred by most of the aeronauts because it allowed them to light up a cigarette midflight.

Among the admirers of the nascent sport was Sir Arthur Conan Doyle, who followed its development with interest, having previously floated (forgive me) the idea of using small balloons or "hydrogen knapsacks" to help lighten pedestrians. He told the Associated Press on March 26, 1927:

> I feel that too much should not be attempted. If the margin between the man's weight and the lifting power is only a few pounds, and huge leaps are made, it will mean a loss of control and be the cause of many accidents. What is needed is to turn the 15-stone man into a 5-stone man, so that he can go on his way swiftly and without fatigue. Better 30-foot strides under control than 100-yard springs where one may be the sport of puffs of wind or unseen obstacles.

The January 1927 issue of *Science and Invention* magazine reported a balloon jumping demonstration in England, declaring its hope that this pastime would soon take the United States by storm, and dreaming of the format competitive events could take:

> Races with balloons of this sort would undoubtedly be great fun and the danger would be very slight. Obstacle races of course would be the most fun because you then bring the advantages

of the balloons into full play. We hope to soon see this sport developed by some American balloon manufacturer in this country.

Frederick S. Hoppin, writing for the August 1927 issue of *Forum*, described the sport as requiring very little practice to master, and being relatively safe:

> The tradition of the dangers of the large balloon has made men provide the jumpers with all kinds of safety devices—bags of sand to further balance the upward pull of the balloon, safety catches to enable the jumper to slip easily out of the harness if, on landing, a sudden gust of wind begins to drag him along with it, and even a rope around the waist attached by its other end to someone on the ground, to keep the jumper from being turned by too strong a gust into the tail of a runaway kite.

However, despite its potential as the transportation of tomorrow and its supposedly low-risk operation, balloon jumping was in fact incredibly dangerous, even for the aeronautical experts pioneering the sport. One such trailblazer was Aircraftman "Brainy," as his men called him, Dobbs, a British parachutist in the Royal Air Force. "A parachute," Dobbs would advise his trainees, "must be so simple that even the highest officer in the Royal Air Force can understand it." Dobbs was a huge fan of balloon jumping, and performed demonstrations to try to kindle public interest. In March 1927, Dobbs was practicing "balloon hopping" at Stag Lane Aerodrome in North London. A nearby officer, Captain Blacker, noticed that Dobbs's leaps were taking him nearer and

Photographs by P and A

PREPARING FOR A JUMP

The "jumping balloonist" is adjusting his ballast and harness before venturing to leave the ground in an initial jump

OVER AN AUTOMOBILE

Here the balloonist is demonstrating his ability to clear obstacles. A single bound carried him over an automobile

The reality of balloon jumping was somewhat
more cumbersome—and dangerous.

nearer to a high-tension cable. "For God's sake, take care," he shouted. "Those are live wires." Dobbs replied, "I'll risk it," and proceeded to jump. He did nearly clear the electrified cables, but unfortunately his feet became entangled, and when he tried to extract himself by grabbing one of the wires he was blown to the ground in a hail of sparks, dying instantly.

Alas, balloon jumpers never quite managed to refine the sport to a level of safety below "frequently lethal," and when stories such as Dobbs's hit the headlines, its popularity was short-lived. Seen in its age of groundbreaking aeronautical innovation and aerial daredevilry, it isn't hard to understand how balloon jumping came into existence, how thrilling it must have been to have the sky open up as a new world to explore. And today, when one finds oneself wedged between sweating strangers in an airless train carriage, it isn't hard to sense the excitement it must have offered its devotees, or feel the regret that it never quite took off.

BARKING OFF SQUIRRELS

While living in Kentucky between 1808 and 1834, the ornithologist John James Audubon observed several rifle sports practiced by North American frontiersmen. "Driving the nail" involved the marksman attempting to hit the head of a nail squarely with a bullet from a hundred paces, driving it into a tree. "Snuffing the candle," another sharpshooting competition, is equally self-explanatory. These, however, were insufficient challenges for the crack shots who desired a moving target, and crosshairs were turned on the surrounding woodland and the great quantities of squirrels, which were so abundant as to be "seen gamboling on every tree around us," according to Audubon.

The creatures were certainly having a rough time of it at the hands of the settlers: in May 1796 the *Kentucky Gazette* carried a report of one hunting party returning from a day's shooting with a tally of 7,941 squirrel kills. "Barking off squirrels" differed from a standard hunt by the simple stipulation that the animal could not be killed with a direct shot. Instead, it was the tree bark to which it clung that was the target, explained Audubon, who accompanied the legendary pioneer Daniel Boone on a squirrel-barking outing:

> Judge of my surprise when I perceived that the ball had hit the piece of bark immediately beneath the squirrel, and shivered it into splinters, the concussion produced by which had killed the animal, and sent it whirling through the air, as if it had been blown by explosion of a powder magazine.

The skill was not just in the precision of the shot but the speed with which one could reload. This offered great competitive sport, an opportunity to gamble, and a Kentucky countryside filled with gunshots and flying squirrels corpses, as hunters emulated the great folk hero Boone. The tails were kept as trophies to be mounted or worn, and the meat thrown into a pot for a frontier stew recipe known as "burgoo."

BARREL JUMPING

If a team of experts was tasked with inventing an activity to most efficiently destroy the human spine, the result would almost certainly resemble the sport of barrel jumping.

Over three hundred years ago, ice skating on the frozen waterways of Holland was a thriving sport, and it was usual to see the skaters attempt to leap over hurdles such as snowdrifts, ridges, and objects deliberately placed on the ice to act as obstacles. While never formally devised as an official sport, fun continued to be had in this way until, in the early twentieth century, the shape of an event began to form. The boundaries of outdoor ice rinks on lakes and rivers were commonly marked out with apple and flour barrels, and speed skaters competed to see who could clear the most barrels in one leap. Speeds of up to thirty miles an hour would be reached before the jumper threw himself into the air feetfirst, with a technique identical to that of a long jumper. This meant, of course, landing in the same manner, directly on the coccyx or hip, with bone-shattering brutality. In the early days this was also done without any form of padding or safety equipment.

An American speed skating champion named Ed Lamy popular-ized the sport. Lamy was known for his showmanship, and his habit of finishing the last lap of a race skating backwards. In 1912 he set a world record of fourteen barrels, a distance of twenty-seven feet eight inches (a feat that earned him a place in *Ripley's Believe It or Not*).

The event then enjoyed a boost in popularity in 1951 when former speed skating champion Irving Jaffee organized the first-ever international tournament at Grossingers Country Club in New York. It was at this time that rules were drawn up; safety equipment, such as helmets and padding for the lower back, was introduced; and the size of the barrels was regulated—a crucial factor in formalizing the sport and having records officially rec-ognized. The Barrel Jumping Championships became an annual event in the United States, with a high number of the contestants

Richard Widmark wins the 1968 Barrel Jumping Championship, clearing sixteen barrels. The former North American speed skating champion from Illinois beat a wide field to take the title. (*Corbis*)

originating from Canada, where the sport had been met with particular enthusiasm since being introduced in 1940.

Barrel jumpers constantly fought for the ultimate recognition of their sport: inclusion in the Olympic calendar. But the governing body was resistant. The Canadian Barrel Jumping Federation even staged a public exhibition at the Lillehammer Games in 1994, but again failed to ignite the interest of the select committee, who feared for the coccyges of an entire generation of impressionable young sports fans. "It appeared to be a brutal sort of sport," a spokesman said. "Nobody really makes it."

BASEBALL WITH CANNON

The forgotten revolutionary of American baseball was, in fact, an Englishman. Charles Howard Hinton was a brilliant man: a prominent mathematician and science fiction writer, he is known for his work on the subject of the fourth dimension and for coining several key words of mathematical vocabulary, including the term "tesseract." After graduating from Balliol College, Oxford, he taught at Uppingham School until, upon being convicted of bigamy,* he was forced to find new employment.

In 1893 he accepted a teaching position at Princeton University's school of mathematics, and it was here that he turned his brilliance to an issue more pressing than the furthering of scientific progress: the sore arm of the baseball pitcher. "Amongst

---

* The result no doubt of growing up under a polygamist father, who once told Hinton's mother: "Christ was the savior of Men but I am the savior of Women, and I don't envy him a bit."

college boys I had noticed many a case of an aspirant who had to relinquish all efforts to make the team because his arm gave out," he wrote in an article for *Harper's Weekly* in 1897. Hinton decided to construct a pitching machine to help with batting practice.

His first design was a catapult with an artificial hand to make the ball spin, but in Hinton's own words, "This device failed altogether in point of accuracy of aim," and so he revisited the drawing board. "At this juncture," he wrote, "it occurred to me that practically whenever men wished to impel a ball with velocity and precision, they drove it out of a tube with powder. Following then the course of history, I determined to use a cannon of a bore which would just hold a baseball . . ."

The machine consisted of a breech-loading rifle action, with a brass tube for a barrel, made telescopic to allow for variation in velocity. The basic mechanism was achieved, but for Hinton the machine would be a success only if it perfectly mimicked the

MECHANICAL PITCHER—EXPERIMENTAL FORM.

Hinton's baseball cannon, as illustrated in *Harper's Weekly*, March 20, 1897.

action of the pitcher—and that meant making the ball curve. Various ideas were explored, including stringing a high-tensile wire across the front of the barrel, but that merely resulted in the field being sprayed with deadly pieces of high-tensile wire. Then he hit on a solution. "The cannon should have fingers," he decided. Small rubber pincers placed in front of the barrel spun the ball upon its release, and curvature was achieved.

The design complete, the pitching cannon was rolled out onto the practice field. However, several inherent problems soon became obvious—the predominant one being that most people don't enjoy being repeatedly shot at. The cannon terrified the batters: the terrific bang and velocity of the projectile invariably caused them instinctively to dive out of the way. In an attempt to solve this, the trigger-man was instructed to signal to the hitter the impending cannon fire by raising his hand before shooting. Later, a wire was hooked up from home plate to the gun's trigger, giving the batter control over the firing by stepping on the plate when he was ready. Even so, this was far from ideal.

A last issue arose with the firing mechanism itself: the gunpowder blast had a tendency to cook and harden the leather surface of the ball, until after a couple of "pitches" it had all the elasticity of a flying brick. The machine also took a while to reload, which slowed the pace of both the practices and the matches in which it was introduced as a novelty feature. The device was too far ahead of its time, and in 1907 Hinton was forced to concede defeat and the invention was retired.

BATTLE-BALL

D r. Dudley Sargent was an American trailblazer in the field of physical conditioning and the promotion of health. In 1881 he founded the Sargent School of Physical Training in Cambridge, Massachusetts, to train teachers in physical education. It was initially open only to women, but men were finally allowed through the doors in 1904. A progressive, Sargent rubbished the Victorian notion that females were at constant risk of fainting; the ladies were free to dress however they wanted, and were keenly encouraged to participate in various programs of demanding physical exercise. These programs were mixtures of various gymnastic activities, and a special sport that Sargent devised himself in 1894: battle-ball.

The recent rise in popularity of athletic sports and the recognition of the value of competitive exercise had inspired the doctor to incorporate other activities in his teaching, but he quickly found a problem: "When we come to look over the list of games, however, that are applicable to the wants of the mass of players, we find the number exceedingly limited," he wrote in a pamphlet at the time. Each major sport appeared to him to have a significant flaw: baseball and soccer required a large amount of open space to play, and time to develop the necessary skills; tennis, too, was viewed as demanding unreasonable amounts of time and area.

So he decided to devise his own sport, and made a list of its requirements. It should be interesting enough to maintain enthusiasm, and vigorous enough to encourage good circulation and respiration; it should be able to be played indoors, in a 1,200-square-foot gymnasium; it should be simple to grasp

A battle-ball match in progress. This illustration originally appeared in *The Battle-ball Rulebook* by D. A. Sargent, M.D., in 1894.

and work as much of the body as possible. Battle-ball was the result—"a game which embraces at once some of the features of bowling, base-ball, cricket, foot-ball, hand-ball and tennis." The rules are so numerous and complex as to require a background in forensic accountancy to untangle, but essentially the teams utilized a range of approved tactics to hurl a rubber football past (or through) their opponents and across their goal line during a series of baseball-style innings, without ever committing the ultimate Victorian transgression of bodily contact.

As well intended as it was, the game failed to generate the level of enthusiasm he had hoped, perhaps because its scientific design could only coldly mimic the heart of its components. After publishing the game's rule book and engaging in a brief campaign to have it adopted into the curriculum of neighboring colleges, Sargent abandoned the sport to focus on teaching his female students the intricacies of German and Swedish gymnastics.

BEAR-BAITING AND THE BEAR GARDEN

Today, a walk along the southern bank of the Thames between Blackfriars Bridge and London Bridge is a peaceful and relatively bloodless affair. But centuries ago the Bankside sky was filled with the roars and cheers of a thousand-strong audience packed into a three-story building, the existence of which has long since been swept from memory. The Bear Garden, or Paris Garden, was one of several venues where the sport of bear-baiting took place, in which bears and other exotic creatures were set upon by packs of dogs (usually the vicious and muscular English bulldog) for the amusement of a paying crowd. The tormenting of bears as a spectacle came into popular practice in the thirteenth century, and remained a common fixture right up to the nineteenth century.

The bears native to Britain had long been hunted to extinction, and so for the baitings the animals were imported from overseas, particularly from Russia. Highly valuable, they were well looked after and housed in great number—during his time in England, Desiderius Erasmus wrote ca. 1500 of "many herds of bears maintained in the country for the purpose of baiting." A list from the Bear Garden of 1590 contains the names of some of the resident bears, which included Jermey, Danyell, Tom Hunkes, and Harry of Tame; while records from 1638 mention George of Cambridge, Don John, Ben Hunt, and Kate of Kent.

In preparation for the fights, the bears were declawed, had their canine teeth removed, and were then tied to a post in the center of the pit by an iron collar, leg chain, or, most commonly in Elizabethan times, a nose ring.*

The animal was taunted by an attendant with a stick to work it up into a rage, and then a pack of half a dozen or so dogs was released into the arena. The bear had to defend itself with blunt swipes as the animals lunged, jeered on by the crowd, most of whom had money riding on the result. Victory for the dogs was declared if one managed to sink its teeth into the bear (though it was a common occurrence, the death of the bear was not required). A steward would then have to run into the mêlée and prize the dog's jaws open with a pole to release the animal.

An Elizabethan court official and chronicler named Robert Laneham described such a scene in 1575:

> It was a sport very pleasant to see, to see the bear, with his pink eyes, tearing after his enemies' approach; the nimbleness and wait of the dog to take his advantage and the force and experience of the bear again to avoid his assaults: if he were bitten in one place how he would pinch in another to get free; that if he were taken once, then by what shift with biting, with clawing, with roaring, with tossing and tumbling he would work and wind himself from them; and when he was loose to shake his ears twice or thrice with the blood and the slaver hanging about his physiognomy.

---

* In *Humorous Lovers*, printed in 1617, the Duke of Newcastle equates the horror of bear-baiting with that of matrimony: "I fear the wedlock ring more than the bear does the ring in his nose."

Paul Hentzner provides a similar description in 1598, adding that the whipping of a blinded bear was a favorite variation of the sport.

Bear-baiting had many fans: one occasion in 1538 was so popular that over a thousand people crammed into the auditorium; the grandstand collapsed, killing many of the spectators. Henry VIII had a pit built at Whitehall; Sir Walter Raleigh claimed that the Southwark Bear Gardens were one of London's unmissable sights; and Elizabeth I allegedly attended a bear-baiting display featuring thirteen bears in 1575. When the suggestion was raised in parliament to ban the sport from taking place on Sundays, she intervened to save it. She even created the crown office of Master of Bears, which included a daily salary of one shilling and four pence.

Action was also taken to protect bear-baiting from a burgeoning threat: the theater. Theatrical performances were proving to be so popular in 1591 that a law was passed decreeing all theaters be closed on Thursdays, so as not to neglect bull- and bear-baiting events in the gardens. The irony of this was that the pits had been instrumental in theater's early success: the pit owners had sought extra revenue by erecting stages in the pit and allowing dramatic performances, which then gained sufficient popularity to encourage the opening of dedicated theaters.

Extra revenue was also sought by varying the species baited in the bear pits. An English leather vendor and preacher named Praise-God Barebone (1598–1679) invented a form of baiting in which a monkey was strapped to the back of a pony, which was in turn tied to a stake. The pair were then savaged by dogs. It was witnessed by a visiting Spaniard named Hernan Fuentes, who wrote: "To see the animal kicking amongst the dogs, with the screaming of the ape, beholding the curs hanging from the ears and neck of the pony, is very laughable."

Though it was to enjoy such popularity for centuries, bear-baiting was met with criticism early on. Some felt it was distracting the people from more useful practices like archery, but the most vocal were the Puritan critics: Philip Stubbes, in his 1583 *Anatomie of Abuses*, condemned it, lamenting:

> Is not the baiting of a bear, besides that it is a filthy, stinking and loathsome game, a dangerous and perilous exercise? . . . What Christian heart can take pleasure to see one poor beast to rend and tear and kill another, and all for his foolish pleasure?

Attitudes slowly began to sway. The diarist John Evelyn wrote in 1670: "I most heartily weary of the rude and dirty pastime, which I had not seen, I think, in twenty years before." An attempt to ban the sport was made in 1724, but it continued in slightly more regulated form, though losing none of its brutality, as an advertisement from that year indicates:

> A mad bull to be dress'd up with fireworks and turned loose in the game place. Likewise a dog to be dress'd up with fireworks over him and turned loose with the bull amongst the men in the ground. Also a bear to be turn'd loose at the same time; and a cat to be ty'd to the bull's tail!

Toward the end of the eighteenth century the voices denouncing animal-baiting had grown louder, and other sports that

This illustration from a 1796 edition of the *Sporting Magazine* was captioned: "The country squire taking a peep at Charley's theatre Westminster where the performers are of the old school."

involved a fairer fight, such as boxing, offered greater appeal. The Society for the Prevention of Cruelty to Animals was founded in 1824, and finally in 1835 the Cruelty to Animals Act was passed, and the sport was brought to an end.

BEAT THE CAT OUT OF THE BARREL

This was a medieval sport played across Europe but most commonly associated with Denmark. There it was known as *Slå katten of tønden*, and was played as a part of Fastelavn, or Carnival, which takes place the Sunday or Monday after Ash Wednesday. It is thought that the tradition arrived in Denmark with the Dutch farmers who migrated to the island of Amager near Copenhagen on the invitation of King Christian II (1481–1559). Fastelavn is

This illustration from ca. 1860 shows how this was
a sport for men and women alike.

a celebration of the start of Lent, and in the Middle Ages it featured games suitable for all the family, including stuffing a black
cat into a barrel, hanging it from a tree, and beating it with sticks
until the wood shattered. The cat would tumble out, only to be
chased down and bludgeoned to death. The person who managed
to break the base of the barrel and send the cat tumbling out was
crowned *kattedronning* (Cat Queen), while the title of *kattekonge*
(Cat King) went to whoever smashed away the last piece of the
barrel. The sport originated as a superstitious ritual to purge bad
omens, and is one of many examples of cats suffering from their
association with witchcraft, devilry, and misfortune. A form of

the game is still played in Denmark, although the barrel is now filled with sweets and carries only the image of a cat painted on the side.

The game was also popular in Scotland. Records show that, up until the eighteenth century, in Perth and Kelso cats were inserted into barrels filled with soot, which were closed up and hung in a tree. Here, too, the winner was the batsman who succeeded in breaking open the barrel. A historian of the area wrote in 1836 about the game being played to a vile conclusion at Perth's Midsummer Market, noting:

> [The men] rode through, giving the barrel a stroke; and the man that broke the barrel and let out the cat (by which he received a plentiful quantity of soot about his ears) gained the prize. The poor cat was then tossed about amongst the mob, which put an end to its future usefulness. Its remains afforded rude sport to the youths.

BIRD-BATTING

The earliest known use of the phrase "beating around the bush" can be found in an anonymous medieval poem, *Generydes— A Romance in Seven-line Stanzas* (ca. 1440), the only copy of which can be found in the library of Trinity College, Cambridge:

> *Butt as it hath be sayde full long agoo,*
> *Some bete the bussh and some the byrdes take.*

More than five hundred years later the phrase is still employed in its original sense, but even more remarkable is the sport that inspired its coining. Over the years the pursuit of fowling has taken many different forms, with huntsmen incorporating a range of tactics and equipment, including snares, nets, guns, crossbows, bows and arrows, slings, baits, pitfalls, pipe calls, hides (see Hidden Hunting), dogs, and decoys. But there was also a lesser-known form of avicide known as "bird-batting."

Also called "bat-fowling" or "bat-folding," this was a fruitful form of hunting in the days before firearms, in which an evening's venture would yield droves of dead or captured field and forest birds. Done during the dark nights of winter, the rare sport exploited the hypnotic susceptibility, curiosity, and general stupidity of roosting birds. There were two forms of bird-batting: the first involved the use of both large nets and smaller handheld versions that resembled tennis rackets; for the other, the participant relied solely on his wooden club. Expeditions equipped with nets were usually formed of two or three people, each brandishing their own lantern made from strips of linen soaked in tallow, a substance rendered from animal fat which produced a steady light when ignited. Upon coming across a sleeping flock, the companions would rustle the surrounding bushes as one man lit his lantern and held it aloft. Fascinated by the glow, the birds would dopily approach.

"The birds will be so amazed," wrote Joseph Strutt in 1801, "that when you come near them, they will turn up their white bellies: your companions shall then lay their nets quietly upon them, and take them." Sometimes a crossbow was also used to bag

This illustration taken from a 1653 book by Johann Conrad Aitinger shows the incredible lengths people went to in bird-batting.

the ones out of reach of the nets, despite their long handles, while clap nets baited with corn were also a common sight.

Bird-batting without nets was most successful when conducted by a mob of fifteen or so hunters. A third of the men were equipped with long poles tipped with bound bundles of straw, cloth, or resin. Another third were tasked with lighting these ends and using their own staffs to club the creatures as they appeared. These poles should be "very rough and bushy at the upper ends, of which the willow, byrche or long hazell are best," advises Gervase Markham in his *Hunger's Prevention* (1621). The final third used their poles to beat the bushes and treetops to startle the quarry out of their slumber, "so that they may be knocked down very easily: and thus you may find good diversion for dark nights."

An alternative luring technique involved with bat-fowling was known as "low-belling." Often used in conjunction with lanterns if hunting at night, the low bell was rhythmically rung by a member of the hunting party as the other men followed with their nets raised. The bells were handheld, and their deep, hollow sounds were chosen for their hypnotic effect. According to *The Sportsman's Dictionary: or, The Gentleman's Companion* (1778), "The sound of the low-bell causes the birds to lie close, and not to stir while you lay the net over them." For those who preferred to hunt solo, the practice was to carry a low bell in one hand, and in the other a net about two feet broad and three long; or, alternatively, the low bell could be tied to one's belt, and one's motion would be used to ring it. "But you must continue to ring the bell," advises Strutt, "for, if the sound shall cease, the other birds, if there be any more near at hand, will rise up and fly away."

"Thus you may spend as much of the night as is darke," wrote Markham, "for longer is not convenient, and doubtlesse you shall find much pastime, and take great store of birds . . ."

Bat-fowling survived into the early twentieth century, when it was used by gamekeepers to gather stock for trap shoots, until the sport was banned by Parliament in 1921. However, it lived on in an alternative existence—"bat-fowling" became a label for a form of con-artistry. Also practiced at dusk, the villainous bat-fowler would approach the doorway of a respectable shop and act as though he had dropped a valuable ring, lighting a candle as he pretended to look for it. The apprentice shopkeeper would become curious and go to find out what was happening. The bat-fowler would explain, and then "accidentally" snuff out his candle. After begging the young man to relight it for him, he then robbed the shop while the assistant went to find a match.

BLOODLESS DUELING

There was a time when dueling was the favored method of European aristocrats to restore honor, or gain "satisfaction," when slighted. For some it was a sport, known as "blazing" or "smelling powder." "A duel was considered a necessary piece of a young man's education," wrote the Irish memoirist Sir Jonah Barrington (1760–1834). "The first two questions always asked when he proposed for a lady-wife were: 'What family is he of? Did he ever blaze?'" Richard Daly, the manager of the Crow Street Theatre in Dublin, dueled sixteen times in one year. Another "fire-eater" was Brian Maguire, an Irish trader who was so fond of the activity that he would throw dirt from his window onto the heads of passersby to provoke a new challenge. Crow Ryan of Carrickon-Suir was famous for challenging every person he met. There have even been four British prime ministers to have engaged in duels: William Petty, William Pitt the Younger, George Canning, and the Duke of Wellington, two of whom fought while in office (Pitt and Wellington). In America there was sitting vice president Aaron Burr killing the former secretary of the Treasury Alexander Hamilton in a duel. It could safely be said that, for most people, the idea of voluntarily being shot at with pistols lacks a fundamental enticement to overcome the notion of being shot at with pistols. Not so for these characters, and not so for the Parisian duelists of the early 1900s who, long after lethal dueling was outlawed, used .44 caliber pistols to fire bullets made of wax and fat at each other in a sport referred to as "bloodless dueling."

This was the game of choice for those searching for the thrill of combat without the inconvenience of mortal wounding, and

A duel with wax bullets in New York, October 27, 1909. (*Bain Collection*)

its popularity quickly spread across the continent and to America, where demonstration matches were held in 1909 at the New York Athletic Club and the Carnegie Hall Gymnasium. The duelists wore heavy overalls and protective masks with a panel of plate glass over the eyes, with hand guards attached to the pistols. Fired at a distance of thirty feet, the bullet could penetrate one hundred pages of a telephone book, and indeed the duels were often prefaced with this stunt for effect before the duelists took up position with an intervening space of about sixty feet.

Despite these precautions, the risk factor was still high. Walter Winans, an American champion horseman and marksman, demonstrated wax dueling at a Franco-British exposition in 1908. He warned of the dangers afterwards in an interview with the *London Sketch*:

Anyone used to shooting dangerous game and driving in trot-
ting competitions does not notice the amount of danger in
these pistol competitions . . . There is, however, a very real danger in this wax, or rather composition-bullet, shooting at each
other. When I first tried it several years ago, I shot out the soft
piece of flesh connecting the thumb and forefinger of the right
hand of M. Gustave Voulquin, the well-known French sporting
writer, and he tells me it still pains him when he has a lot of
writing to do.

The sport was simply too perilous, and experts including Winans
recommended that the use of iron targets in the shape of men be
used instead.

Incidentally, there is something of a tradition in France of
fighting duels in an unusual manner. On May 3, 1808, M. de
Grandpré and M. de Pique settled a quarrel over the affections of
a dancer named Mademoiselle Tirevit by dueling from the baskets
of hot air balloons two thousand feet above Paris. De Pique fired
first and missed; Grandpré scored a hit that collapsed de Pique's
balloon and sent it crashing to the rooftops below, killing him and
his second. In 1830, the French writer Sainte-Beuve challenged
Paul-François Dubois, one of the owners of *Le Globe.* The duel
took place during heavy rain, and Sainte-Beuve held his umbrella
aloft throughout, announcing that although dying was a possibility he was damned if he was going to get wet while doing so. And
in 1843 two Frenchmen fought a brutal duel by hurling their
weapon of choice at each other's head: for this occasion, the men
had selected billiard balls.

BONE SKATING

When examining the history of the sport, the etymology of ice-skating is particularly illuminating. The English word "skate" is derived from the Dutch word *schaats*, from the Old French *eschasse*, meaning "stilt"; but an even older Dutch word for skate is *schenkel*, which means "leg bone."

In January 1874 a pair of ice skates was presented to the British Archaeological Association. They were "two British skates of bone," which had been discovered on the site of the old Fleet River in Blackfriars, London. A month later, two more bone skates, one smoothly polished, the other in the process of manufacture, were found; and four months after that, Mr. Loftus Brock exhibited "a fine bone skate about a foot long with a flat polished surface, of prehistoric date," which had been found on the grounds of the ancient church of St. Benet Sherehog in Bucklersbury. Each discovery matched the description of the sport as practiced in London provided by contemporary historians, the most respected of whom was William Fitzstephen (died ca. 1190), chronicler of London in the twelfth century, whose description of the skaters paints a particularly vivid image:

> When that great moor which washed Moorfields, at the north wall of the city, is frozen over, great companies of young men go to sport upon the ice, and bind to their shoes bones, as the legs of some beasts; and hold stakes in their hands, headed with sharp iron, which sometimes they stick against ice; and these men go on with speed, as doth a bird in the air, or darts shot from some warlike engine. Sometimes two men set themselves

at a distance, and run one against another, as it were at tilt, with these stakes; where with one or both parties are thrown down, not without some hurt to their bodies; and after their fall, by reason of their violent motion, are carried a good distance one from another; and wheresoever the ice doth touch their heads, it rubs off the skin and lays it bare; and if one fall upon his leg or arm, it is usually broken; but young men, being greedy of honour and desirous of victory, do thus exercise themselves in counterfeit battles that they may bear the brunt more strongly when they come to it in good earnest.

In the fourteenth century, the Dutch replaced the bone blades with iron runners attached to wooden platform shoes, and so began the evolution that would lead to the design of contemporary ice skates. In Britain, during the intensely cold medieval period known as the Little Ice Age (from 1350 to about 1850), the River Thames occasionally froze with such density that "frost fairs" were held on its surface, featuring horse races, puppet plays, and, of course, ice-skating on bones. (In 1841, during one such violent freeze, an elephant was even persuaded to cross the river below Blackfriars Bridge.) The famous Restoration diarists, John Evelyn and Samuel Pepys, both record witnessing the skating that occurred in St. James's Park on December 1, 1662, when metal-bladed skates were first introduced in a public demonstration. Evelyn wrote:

Having seen the strange and wonderful dexterity of the sliders on the new canal in St. James's Park, performed before their majesties by divers gentlemen, and others with Scheetes after the manner of the Hollanders, with what swiftnesse they passe, how suddainely they stop in full carriere upon the ice, I went home by water, but not without exceeding difficulties, the Thames being frozen, greate flakes of ice incompassing our boate.

Watching elsewhere in the park was Pepys, whose entry reads: "St. James's Park, Dec. 1, 1662. Over the Park, where I first in my life, it being a great frost, did see people sliding with their skeates, which is a very pretty art."

In 2007 a research team from Oxford University traced the origins of ice-skating back to Finland in 2000 BC. The skaters fashioned their blades from the leg bones of horses, boring holes into each end and attaching them with leather straps. The bone

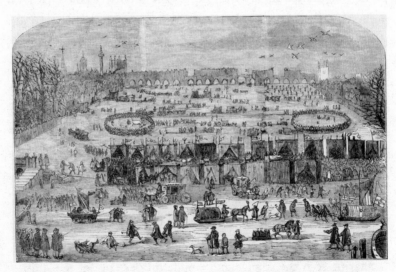

A frost fair on the Thames in 1683 during the reign of Charles II, taken from the *Illustrated London News* 1855. Sir Christopher Wren's Monument, completed in 1677 after the Great Fire, can be seen at top left.

blades met with less friction than modern skates because of the coating of residual fat, and the skaters would use sticks to propel themselves with ease across the frozen rivers and small lakes of the southern Finnish landscape. Dr. Federico Formenti of the Oxford team told the BBC that from personal experience skating on bone was "quite good fun."

BOW-AND-ARROW GOLF

A cry of "fore" would have come too late here. Also known as "archery golf," this was a sport in which golfers and archers competed against each other on the same course. Instances of this wildly dangerous game began to be recorded in America in the 1920s. It took place mostly in winter, when the arrows would do less damage to the frozen turf, and the number of players was kept to a limit of four (presumably because a game of several groups playing through would quickly resemble a scene from *Braveheart*). Archers often took a ten-point handicap when playing against regular golfers, and, just as in golf, the lowest score won. Everyone teed off from the same spot, with the second shot being taken from wherever the first arrow hit the ground. Three different types of arrows were used: a flight arrow (light with short fletching) for the first drive; a medium approach arrow (heavily feathered with a long point); and a flu-flu (heavy, blunt point) for "putting." The "hole" for the archer was usually a tennis ball perched on top of a can, or another similarly small target, such as a small plate-sized disc pinned to a tree or stand.

Despite the modern setting, the game in fact closely resembled one of the oldest forms of competitive archery, "roving marks," played by medieval English longbowmen (including Henry VIII) as practice for warfare. The men would move in large groups through the countryside, picking out targets on the fly to dictate their course.

Archery golf had many fans and was often used as a promotional stunt for the launching of new courses; it even featured in the Miss Florida beauty pageant held in Sarasota in 1958. A notable champion of the sport, and indeed of archery as a whole, was the inimitable Howard Hill, whose list of sporting achievements could fill this book alone. A prolific hunter often referred to as "the best archer who ever lived," Hill brought his skills to

Donna Jeanne Hoogerhyde displays the archery skills that helped her win the Ivanhoe Cup in 1952. (*Corbis*)

Hollywood in the 1930s, where he performed all the archery in the films *The Adventures of Robin Hood* (1938), *They Died with Their Boots On* (1941), *Buffalo Bill* (1944), and many others. He also won seven National Archery Golf Tournaments and wrote the first set of archery golf rules in 1928.

Bow-and-arrow golf matches were held until the late 1970s, when, to the relief of groundsmen everywhere, health and safety regulators began to balk at a sport with the potential to perforate its players.

BOXING ON HORSEBACK

In the early twentieth century, one of the most renowned and fearsome welterweights on the European boxing scene was a forty-two-year-old African-American named Bobby Dobbs. With prizefighting opportunities in the US drying up, Dobbs, like many fighters, had ventured abroad in search of steady work. Powerful yet elegantly built, with a striking litheness, Dobbs enhanced his intriguing story by exaggerating his age to journalists, and after fighting his way around England he decided to try his luck in Berlin. Boxing had recently begun to be met with enthusiasm in Germany, and Dobbs's arrival catalyzed the craze. On December 2, 1910, he defeated fellow American Dick Green in the first major prizefight held in Germany, and he was greeted with national fame, which he cunningly harnessed to help found the Anglo-American Boxing Club in Berlin. Soon, though, German fervor for the sport began to ebb, and Dobbs was forced to search for fresh and exciting ways to present his sport. Working with another trainer at the club, an Anglo-German named Joe Edwards, the men created the sport known as "boxing on horseback."

The game was conducted in much the same way as regular boxing (aside from the thousand-pound animals bucking beneath the fighters), in keeping with the Queensberry rules: a ring was roughly marked out, the action was fought in timed rounds, no hugging or wrestling was allowed, and no one else was permitted in the ring other than the referee. A fighter was declared the loser if he was thrown from his steed by a punch and was unable to remount within ten seconds. The men fought bare-breasted and wore four-ounce boxing gloves, in observance of the traditional rules but to the detriment of gripping the reins. As a result, rounds consisted of only sporadic clashes, for the contenders devoted most of their efforts to the challenge of maneuvering the horses alongside each other. The horses, meanwhile, were chosen for their resistance to flight, and were dressed in protective leather guards.

Dobbs and Edwards introduced the game to the Berlin club members who—though initially baffled—loved it. Among the 369 male and female members* was a German cavalry officer who was so taken with the sport that he brought it to the attention of his superiors, citing it as a useful martial training exercise. "The new sport will be valuable for the soldier on horseback in

---

* The seventy or so female members of Berlin's Anglo-American Boxing Club appear to have been particularly formidable. The "ladies of high standing" were reported by the *New York Times* in 1912 to have "recently had a battle of arms with the Berlin police, who attempted to interfere with their boxing bouts in the open of the Tiergarten, and are said to have come off victorious."

time of war," it was explained, "as when he loses his weapons he will have to fall back on his natural means of defense."

So positive was the initial reaction that the club decided to stage a public demonstration. Berlin's Tiergarten is an area steeped in sporting history, once serving as the hunting ground of the Electors of Brandenburg; but, perhaps most impressively, on July 4, 1912, it was the setting of a grand boxing on horseback tournament. Among the witnesses to the spectacle were members of the imperial family, the American ambassador John G. A. Leishman, and high-ranking German cavalry officers, all cheering on the boxing club fighters as they galloped around the grounds with limited navigational control.

Sadly for Dobbs and his Anglo-American Boxing Club, the new pugilism failed to spark either public or military enthusiasm, and although it enjoyed brief international popularity as an

This boxing on horseback contest took place at the Culver Road Armory in Rochester, New York, in 1922. (*Albert R. Stone Negative*)

exhibition event at fairs and circuses, it soon disappeared. Dobbs returned to America and spent the rest of his time training fighters and continuing to box, despite promoters' reluctance to book him due to his relatively advanced age, something he overcame by competing anonymously as "The Masked Marvel."

BULL-RUNNING

Come all you bonny boys, who love to bait the bonny bull,
Who take delight in noise, and you shall have your bellyful.
On Stamford's town Bull-running Day, we'll shew you such right gallant play,
You never saw the like, you'll say, as you shall see at Stamford.

The Bullard's Song

Today the Spanish city of Pamplona plays host to the most famous bull-running event in the world, the *encierro* of the San Fermín festival held in July, which attracts more than one million visitors annually. These include thousands of British tourists, some of whom might be surprised to learn that the exotic spectacle they have traveled to see took place in their own country for more than seven hundred years, until the tradition ended in 1839.

During the reign of King John (1199–1216), William de Warenne, 5th Earl of Surrey, watched from the battlements of a castle in Stamford as two bulls fought in a nearby meadow. The town butchers arrived and, in an attempt to separate the animals, sent their dogs into the fracas. One of the bulls bolted and headed for town. The baron leapt on his horse and gave chase, and enjoyed the pursuit so much that he gave the meadow to the butchers of Stamford, on the proviso that the chase should be held every year on that date, November 13.

For centuries, the tradition was kept. Each year the streets were blocked off with wagons, and a bull was "irritated by hats being thrown at him, and other means of annoyance" (*The Book of Days*, 1864). The tips of its horns were cut off, as were its ears and tail; its body was rubbed down with soap to make it harder to catch, and finally pepper was blown up its nose to infuriate the poor beast. When it came time for the barricade to be removed, it was ready to run. As it barreled down the streets, the crowd of men, women, children, and dogs took off after it (in a reversal of roles to the run of Pamplona, in which the bulls are the pursuers). "Hivie, shivie, tag and rag," wrote William Hone in *The Every-Day Book* of 1830, "men, women and children of all sorts and sizes, with all the dogs in the town, promiscuously run after him with their bull-clubs scattering dirt in each others' faces, as when Theseus and Pirithous conquered Hell and punished Cerberus."

The animal was chased from the town until it came to the bridge that crossed the River Welland. This was a stage in the event known as "bridging the bull." The crowds approached from both ends, trapping the animal. Together they wrestled with it until they succeeded in throwing it over the side and into the river. The bull usually managed to swim to the bank and drag itself onto dry land, where it was now in the original meadow bequeathed to the butchers. It was then baited with dogs and slaughtered, for it was thought that terror improved the flavor of the meat, which was sold cheaply to the townsfolk for their supper that evening. Any bull that avoided being thrown into the river was given a reprieve.

An illustration by Theodore Lane of a bull being baited, taken
from Pierce Egan's *Book of Sports and Mirror of Life: Embracing
the Turf, the Chase, the Ring, and the Stage* (1832).

The tradition was cherished by the people of Stamford: one
mayor who died in 1756 left money to ensure its continuation,
and records show that even the church wardens annually contributed to the cost. Over the centuries several attempts were made
by authorities to abolish the sport, but these were met with fierce
resistance and, occasionally, open defiance. In 1788 the town's
mayor instigated a ban, and in the following year he enlisted the
help of a troop of dragoons to enforce it. When his edict was
again flouted by the citizenry, he ordered the guards to intervene.
The officer in charge refused; the townsfolk were merely walking
peacefully along a highway. The mayor declared that the soldiers
were therefore useless, to which the officer agreed and dismissed
his men, who promptly joined in the procession.

In 1833 the recently founded Society for the Prevention of Cruelty to Animals protested the Stamford bull run, but this merely

galvanized the people into keener participation. "Who or what is this London society," they asked, "that, usurping the place of constituted authorities, presumes to interfere with our ancient amusement?" Finally, in 1839, a force of soldiers and policemen was sent to prevent the run taking place, and the people relented when it was revealed that the cost of this and any future such deployment would be passed to them, an amount of more than £600.

CAR VS. BULL

I t was a simple idea, but like so many simple ideas it turned out that there was a *reason* why no one else had done it.

Bayonne has the longest bullfighting history of any city in France, and in 1901 a capacity crowd gathered in the nearby Plaza de Toros for a much-publicized bullfight organized by Henri Deutsch de la Meurthe, a wealthy petrochemical tycoon. Deutsch de la Meurthe was a man with a pioneering spirit: the year before he had announced the Deutsch de la Meurthe prize, offering 100,000 francs to the man who could design a flying machine capable of a return flight from Parc de Saint-Cloud to the Eiffel Tower in thirty minutes.*

---

* The prize was won by the Brazilian aeronaut Alberto Santos-Dumont, who made the trip in twenty-nine minutes and thirty seconds, despite suffering engine trouble that forced him to clamber outside the gondola midflight without a safety harness to restart the engine. This was after a failed first attempt that had resulted in his airship crashing into the Trocadero Hotel, leaving the airshipman dangling over the side of the building and having to be rescued by the Paris fire department. On being awarded the prize, he gave half his winnings to his crew and the rest to the city's poor.

To the Bayonne citizenry, Deutsch de la Meurthe had promised a form of bullfighting never before seen. As usual the *caballero de plaza*, a local hero named Ledesma, entered the arena on a steed, except in this instance the "steed" was a twelve-cylinder armor-plated Peugeot driven by Deutsch de la Meurthe's personal chauffeur, M. Chevrin. The automobile toured the arena with Ledesma the *torero* waving his saber from the passenger seat. They then took their position, and a hush fell over the crowd as the bull was released into the stadium. The animal and the automobile faced off. A cry went out from Ledesma; Chevrin threw it into first and the car lurched forward. In response, the bull scraped its hoof along the sand, gave a great snort, and, in the words of the London *Times* journalist covering the event, "turned tail and fled." This was something Deutsch de la Meurthe and his *caballero* had not expected. Nevertheless, Ledesma was determined, and he ordered Chevrin to pursue the terrified bull as it swerved and skidded its way around the arena. Despite the lack of combat, the crowd loved it. After the bull tried to leap over the fencing into the first row, six successive bulls were brought out in the hope that one would attempt to charge the Peugeot, but each animal was as petrified as the first, and eventually the match was abandoned.

CAT-BURNING

As previously evidenced by the game of "beat the cat out of the barrel," throughout history cats have suffered particularly brutal treatment at the hands of men thanks to a superstitious association with the dark arts and ill fortune. Inarguably, though, the most sadistic expression of this cruelty was the medieval French entertainment *brûler les chats*, or cat-burning.

It had long been a custom to throw objects considered to have magical properties into bonfires as an offering to bring good fortune. Unfortunately for cats, they fell into this category, and by the sixteenth century in Paris the burnings had become a more formal tradition, held on festive occasions such as Midsummer Day. People would gather in a public square around a specially constructed scaffold, which towered over a wood pyre. A sack full of cats was then suspended from the scaffold over the logs, and the fire lit. As the flames grew and the animals fell screaming into the blaze to be burned to death, the crowds reveled in the sound as if it were music.

Elsewhere in France, the cat-burning event took on a variety of forms. The Courimauds (cat chasers, from *cour à miaud*) of Saint-Chamond preferred a more active sport: they would douse the cat in flammable liquid, set it alight, and chase it as it streaked through the town. In the city of Metz in the northeastern Lorraine region, dozens of cats in wicker cages were burnt atop bonfires, just as they were in Gap, Hautes-Alpes; while in Burgundy, cats were tied to maypoles that were then set alight—a symbolic burning at the stake. When the flames had been extinguished it was common for people to remove a charred souvenir to take home for good luck. The events were popular with all, from working class to royalty: in 1648 the Sun King, Louis XIV, crowned in a garland of roses, ignited the annual cat bonfire before launching into a dance and heading to a banquet in the town hall. The practice was finally outlawed in 1765.

In a related activity, the ancient Belgian town of Ypres to this day celebrates a medieval festival called the *Kattenstoet* (Festival of Cats), which is traditionally held on the second Sunday of May each year. People line the streets to watch the symbolic procession of costumed jesters and giant feline floats parade through the town before reaching the *Lakenhallen* (Cloth Hall). Up until 1817, it was from the belfry of this building that cats collected from the streets were hurled to their death onto the cobbles below, a custom observed by modern participants who throw stuffed animals down to the crowd. This is then followed by a mock witch burning. The event has become a popular local attraction, and draws thousands of tourists every year.

CENTRIFUGAL BOWLING

In 1885 the arcades beneath the elevated railway in Berlin housed a variety of saloons, stores, and restaurants, turning in a tidy side profit for the owners of the railway line. The proprietor of one of these saloons decided that he could draw in a bigger crowd by installing a bowling alley in his establishment, but faced one significant obstacle: a bowling alley required a room at least seventy-five feet in length, and his saloon was barely half that. To most, perhaps, logic would dictate that the idea be scrapped; but in this instance the proprietor was unwilling to give up on the potentially lucrative venture, and engaged the services of a civil engineer named Kiebitz to solve the problem. Kiebitz visited the site, took measurements, and then ordered a drink to mull it over. By the time he drained his glass, he had conceived a simple yet ingenious solution: if the alley would not fit in the room, then he would bend it until it would. The result was a *U*-shaped, or centrifugal, bowling alley, built with the outer side tilted upwards like the track of a velodrome. The sloped side also minimized the risk of the balls flying off and smashing the glasses of nonbowling patrons. The *U*-shaped design of the alley meant that there was no need for the balls to be returned or fetched; the starting position was beside the pins and so the player had merely to reach over.

An alternative design was introduced in the United States in 1894, intended to combat the scarcity of commercial bowling alleys by making the dream of a bowling alley in every home a reality. This invention, which there was no great rush to buy, involved an alley shaped in a loop-the-loop design, allowing it to fit in the average residence. The intriguing layout may well have diminished accuracy (and the structural integrity of living-

Centrifugal bowling was a simple way to bring the joys of tenpin bowling into the home, as seen in this illustration from *Scientific American*, May 12, 1894.

room walls across America), but surely not the amount of fun that was had.

CHASSE AUX TOILES

In medieval Europe the most exhilarating and respectable form of hunting deer, and other large mammals, was the *chasse par force des chiens*, in which the animal was hunted by dogs with men on horses in hot pursuit. It is also perhaps the image conjured in most minds today when talking of "the hunt." It consisted of eight stages: the quest, in which a gamesman tracked an animal to a general location; the assembly, when the hunting party convened and discussed tactics following a briefing by the gamesman; relays, in which packs of dogs were positioned to intercept the quarry; moving, also known as the "fynding," in which the animal was tracked down; the chase; baying, when the animal had been cornered and was standing its ground, or "at bay," and was killed by a member of the party; the unmaking, when it was skinned and cut apart; and finally the curée, when the dogs were tossed pieces of the meat as a reward. It was a frantic, exhausting, and frequently dangerous activity, as Richard of Normandy found when he was mauled by a stag in the New Forest, which was also the scene of the death of William II a few years later in 1100, when he was shot in the lung by Walter Tirel, a member of his own party. For the vainglorious nobleman, hunting *par force* was all well and good, but it lacked an audience for his heroics, while for many it was simply too much of an exertion.

This illustration from a book by Friedrich von Fleming
depicts a show hunt at a German court, with deer being killed
in an enclosure formed of canvas screens ten feet high.

Sometime in the fifteenth century a solution was found with the *chasse aux toiles*, an alternative "hunt" most popular in France and Germany.

Evolving from the *chasse aux haies* (hunting with hedges as obstacles), vast outdoor enclosures were constructed in the fields adjacent to the forests, using enormous canvas screens called *ancourre*, or *Laufft*, which were sometimes as much as three meters high. A variety of game, including deer and boar, were then driven into this arena by a team of gamesmen. From the stands built around the outside of the pen the nobles would shoot, hack, and hurl spears at the trapped animals, safe behind the screens, with the women of the court cheering them on. Any notions of fair play and sportsmanship were jettisoned in favor of body counts to boast about. Both Louis XIII and Louis XIV were fans of the sport, as was Louis XVI, who practiced a developed form of *chasse aux toiles* known as *hourailleries*, in which the quarry was picked off with matchlock rifles.

In Germany, where forests were thicker and less conducive to hunting *par force*, hunting with canvas screens was so widespread as to be commonly known as the "German hunt." Here the *Laufft* were erected in a figure-eight formation, and the riflemen fired on the animals as they ran around in desperate search of an exit. The bodies were then piled up and carted away. The animals had such little chance of surviving these hunts that they were referred to by the writer Heinrich Döbel in 1783 as *Bestätigtungs-Jagen*, or "confirmed hunts."

The extravagant *chasse aux toiles* fell out of fashion in the late eighteenth century. In France, after the revolution of 1789–99, the canvas was requisitioned for the manufacture of army tents.

CHEETAH GREYHOUND RACING

How a pack of African cheetahs came to race against English greyhounds on a gloomy Essex racetrack in December 1937 is the story of two extraordinary men: Raymond Hook and Kenneth Gandar-Dower.

Hook had an affinity for animals, and from his estate in the Mount Kenya region of East Africa built a business providing exotic wildlife to zoos around the world.* His greatest love, though, was for the cheetah. Having studied the ancient Egyptian hieroglyphics that featured the creatures, he had formed the opinion that the litmus test for the sophistication of a civilization was the level of respect in which cheetahs were held. It was this reverence for the animal, and the effectiveness of his domestication training, that saw Hook become the principal provider of the big cats to Indian royals like the Maharaja of Kolhapur, whose native cheetahs had fallen into extinction.

Hook's method for catching the wild cat is so extraordinary that it is worth including here. The process was witnessed by his friend John Pollard, who wrote:

> Hook . . . divested himself of his belt and stirrup leathers. Armed with these he made a pass like a matador at the creature's head. It growled and spat in sullen fury. But the feint succeeded. For a second its attention was withdrawn from Ali [Hook's assistant], and this was his chance. As he grabbed the tail Hook dived headlong for the cheetah's neck. The next few moments will live in my memory. Having grabbed its neck Hook calmly permitted the cheetah to chew his arm, while he muzzled its jaws with the belt. Two more boys then ran in to assist, and together they succeeded in trussing the writhing cat and tying it to a tree.

---

* This was a passion he prioritized over everything, including his marriage. According to his daughter, Hazel, her mother, Joan, had tried to "instill a sense of responsibility" into her husband, but after nine years of marriage could no longer stand "the chickens sitting under the stairs, the goats bouncing up and down the stairs, and the snakes under the kitchen stove."

When Hook finally rose to his feet he was covered in sweat and blood.

"Only a scratch," he panted, "can't expect to muzzle a wild cheetah without a sustaining a bit of damage."

In 1934 Hook was hired as a guide by a wealthy young English adventurer named Kenneth Gandar-Dower, who had arrived in Africa on a crackpot expedition to find the elusive (and in all probability nonexistent) marozi, a mythical spotted lion rich in rumor but poor in sightings. Gandar-Dower—who, despite possessing little to no aeronautical experience, had made one of the earliest flights from England to India—was captivated by the rugged Hook, a man he described as "ridiculously brown and big, and frighteningly tough." He became infected with Hook's enthusiasm for the cheetah, and over the course of the (fruitless) marozi hunt the men hatched the idea to bring the animals to Britain to create a new racing sport and split the profits.

By December 1936 they had gathered twelve cheetahs and, with two hogs and a rare bongo in tow, set sail for England. Upon arrival, Pongo (alas, not the name of the bongo), Gypsy, Helen, Lewis, and the rest of the cats were taken to an animal quarantine facility where they would stay for six months, adjusting to the English climate. The exotic creatures were then taken to a racetrack in Staines, where they began four months of training while being fed a diet of premium Argentinian beef and wild rabbits. A private demonstration match was staged for invited guests, but it was a disaster: the cats showed little interest in pursuing the raw meat strapped to the electric hare and instead padded over to the bookies, who "scattered like pigeons," according to Briga-

Kenneth Gandar-Dower poses at Hackbridge Kennels in Surrey with
one of the cheetahs he brought back from Kenya. (*Getty Images*)

dier General Alfred Critchley, the owner of the track. This was
enough to convince Hook that the endeavor was doomed, and he
decided to sell his stake to Gandar-Dower, who was undaunted,
convinced that further training was the solution.

And so it was that on December 11, 1937, at Romford Stadium, three races of cheetahs versus greyhounds were held before
a sold-out crowd. The first race starred Helen the cheetah, who,
to the surprise of everyone (including her trainers), got into the
spirit of the day and cleared fifty yards before the dogs had even
left their gates. She bounded over the finish line in first place, covering the 265 yards in 15.86 seconds, smashing the canine record
of 16.01 seconds. Next up were James and Gussie, whose race
was prefaced with the announcement over the Tannoy that if one

should pull ahead, the other might give up. This was exactly what happened. Gussie took the lead and James immediately lost interest, and to the consternation of the spectators decided to investigate the grandstand instead. However, he obediently answered his trainers' calls before reaching the crowd, and the third race went ahead, which saw Lewis finish but fail to beat the track record.

Contrary to how the story is commonly told, the first British cheetah-greyhound race was in fact a considerable success, and Gandar-Dower was moved to form the Cheetah Racing Ltd. company. However, the sport suffered considerably from the restriction that banned gambling on the animals, and in further races the mercurial cheetahs were often completely indifferent to the pursuit, for in the wild they rarely hunt in packs and lack any competitive spirit. The interest of both the public and Gandar-Dower in staging further events waned, and shortly after their last recorded appearance at the Aldershot Show in 1939, World War II began. Gandar-Dower returned to East Africa as a war correspondent, and the experiment was abandoned.

CHUNKEY

The history of the sports and games played by Native Americans offers rich cultural insight, as they were often tied to mythological beliefs. Take, for instance, the game of "chunkey." The game was a serious one, used as practice for battle. A carefully decorated disk, carved from the finest stone and about three inches in diameter, was rolled out along the ground, and when it stopped, two contestants would hurl their spears at wherever it

A painting by George Catlin (1796–1872) from 1832 shows
chunkey being played by the Mandan tribe of North Dakota.
(*Smithsonian American Art Museum*)

had landed. The winner, of course, was the one whose spear came
closest. It was also a recognized tactic to deflect your opponent's
stick with your own, an especially skillful maneuver that drew
admiration from those watching. The game came to an end when
a player accumulated twelve points. It was played in designated
areas called "chunkey yards," usually near the town square or central area, where only the most important activities took place.

The American artist George Catlin saw the game in action in
1832, writing of the version he witnessed:

The game of Tchung-kee [is] a beautiful athletic exercise,
which the Mandan seem to be almost unceasingly practicing
whilst the weather is fair, and they have nothing else of moment
to demand their attention. This game is decidedly their favorite

amusement, and is played near to the village on a pavement of clay, which has been used for that purpose until it has become as smooth and hard as a floor . . . The play commences with two (one from each party), who start off upon a trot, abreast of each other, and one of them rolls in advance of them, on the pavement, a little ring of two or three inches in diameter, cut out of a stone; and each one follows it up with his "tchung-kee" (a stick of six feet in length, with little bits of leather projecting from its sides of an inch or more in length), which he throws before him as he runs, sliding it along upon the ground after the ring, endeavoring to place it in such a position when it stops, that the ring may fall upon it, and receive one of the little projections of leather through it.

No doubt it was fun, but the game also had ceremonial significance—it was connected to a Cherokee myth, that of Wild Boy and his brother, Village Boy. The two are heroes of Midwestern native legend, and usually associated with thunder and lightning. The children were born as twins (a feared phenomenon in the culture) and possessed magical powers. In one version of the story, after their father leaves on a hunt, a monster known as a Caddaja kills their mother while she carries them unborn inside her, and hurls Wild Boy into the wilderness. Both boys survive thanks to their supernatural abilities, and Village Boy is found and cared for by his father. Wild Boy, meanwhile, is forced to fend for himself, and eventually finds his way back to his family by using a chunkey stone to guide his path. According to the Cherokee Heritage Center: "After the Colonial period the game seemed to die out. Reasons for the decline are only speculative. Today, chunkey is not a commonly played game."

CLOSE-QUARTERS BEAR COMBAT

Early labels bestowed on the bear by various cultures reflect the respect with which it was held as an adversary. The Abenaki, Tsimshian, and Tahltan North American Indians referred to him as "cousin," the Penobscot called him "grandfather," the Plains Cree "four-legged human" and "chief's son." The Navajo, Pueblo, and Pima tribes refused to hunt bears altogether, and to the Cheyenne they were considered relatives. To the Siberian Samoyeds, the bear was "old father"; the Carpathian Hutsuls called him "little uncle," and the Laplanders referred to him as "the old man with the fur garment," while he was known as "fur father" and "old claw man" to the Siberian Kets, who respectfully made use of every part of the animal's body—the fat was melted down and used as a salad dressing, the intestines were stretched to serve as windowpanes, and the shoulder blades were used as sickles for trimming grass.

The Siberian hunters of the Lena area had a particularly effective method of catching the bear. According to the nineteenth-century natural historian Anton Benedikt Reichenbach, they attached traps to large rocks:

As the bear majestically strides along, he catches his head and neck in the sling. He looks around and realizes that the heavy stone is hindering his progress. Then in a rage he climbs a peak, seizes the stone in his front paws, and throws it over the cliff. Of course the stone pulls the bear over with it.

Bears were often smoked out of their caves, or frightened out with dogs. Russian and Polish hunters left out pots of honey spiked with alcohol: the bear guzzled it down, and in a drunken state was easily killed. According to the *Mahawansa*, the ancient text of the Sinhalese people of Sri Lanka, in that part of the world a type of lasso was used to catch bears. It consisted of a rope with a noose and metal ring called a *narachana*. A lasso was also the equipment of choice for the Scandinavian and Lapp bear hunters.

In Europe the animal was hunted with dogs, an activity that was so prevalent in Britain that the bear was hunted to extinction as early as AD 1000. One weapon used in the medieval European pursuit of the bear was the curved short sword that could be employed to hack away foliage and also serve as a backup weapon. A scene in one of the Devonshire tapestries of ca. 1425–50 in the Victoria and Albert Museum shows how this could be useful: a cornered bear falls upon a prostrate hunter, who in desperation thrusts upwards into the beast's belly. (What isn't shown, however, is whether the man then survived being crushed by a thousand pounds of dead bear.) Other precautions were also taken: a book of "genuine secret hunting arts" published in the early eighteenth century recommended that bear hunters smear themselves with lion fat, for "as soon as they smell this, they flee," as presumably did everything else with a nose.

Stradanus produced several illustrations of bear hunts, engraved in 1578. In these, hunters on horseback armed with

lances drive the animals toward men waiting with nets. Tangled
in the mesh, the bears were then killed with thick spears that featured crossbars below the blade to stop it going too deep and ruin-
ing the fur, and to prevent the creature, insensitive to pain because
of its rage, from charging along the spear and killing the wielder.
The most striking of Stradanus's images is the scene in which men
in armor take on the bears with short swords. In the background
can be seen the rest of the hunting party, ready with spears, watching the battle. While taking into consideration the fact that these
illustrations were based on secondhand accounts passed to the
artist, the imagery contains many accurate details. Though clearly
hyperbolic, the hunting of bears has always been considered a test
of mettle, and it isn't hard to imagine enthusiastic young hunters
relying on a short sword for the kill, to prove valiancy.

Usually, though, the beast was chased with dogs until cornered. In Walter de Milemete's *De Nobilitatibus, Sapientiis, et
Prudentiis Regum* (1326), several paintings show bears and lions
being attacked with the long medieval sword. Broad and double-
edged, it was a powerful blade that could be thrust through mail
and plate armor, requiring two hands on the handle to take the
impact. However, the sword was dangerously short for the killing
blow—it brought the swordsman within range of claws and teeth,
and the blade often snapped. Huntsmen with spears were given
the job of finishing off the bear; their weapons were stouter than
the standard spear, seven feet long, with some possessing blades
of a further two feet. This was the procedure until the enormous
"hand-and-a-half sword" was developed, which had a reinforced
blade of such great length that a hunter on horseback could slay a
large animal without dismounting. Illustrations of German hunt-

ing scenes of the sixteenth century show the men equipped with the weapon. In India, the bear was hunted on horseback with short spears with broad blades, which the men wielded from the saddle and hurled like javelins in a sport known as bear-sticking. After the bear population declined, the wild boar was targeted instead (see Pig-Sticking).

Between the seventeenth and nineteenth centuries, harpoon crews of European whaling ships would often turn their attention to surrounding polar bears in the event of a fruitless whale hunt. The animals were speared by barbed lances and dragged to the ship by rope, which for good luck was decorated with sweethearts' ribbons and garters.

The introduction of firearms sealed the fate of many native bear populations, especially when the technique of driving the prey en masse toward the hunter became popular in place of the chase. This was particularly true in Germany, home to two of the most prolific mass animal dispatchers, the Electors of Saxony, Johann Georg I (1585–1656) and Johann Georg II (1613–1680). The grand hunting events of the princes brought a combined tally of over 79,000 red deer, 50,000 wild boar, 6,000 wolves, and 500 bears.

COCK-SHYING AND OTHER POULTRY-BASED BLOOD SPORTS

It wasn't always coconuts that perched atop the stands of the shy at fairs. In the fourteenth and fifteenth centuries in England, it was a grave concern that ball sports and other frivolities would distract people from the practice of activities that had the dual benefit of military training. At a time when the country's safe-keeping relied on a population of able bowmen, it was a requirement that a longbow and arrows be kept in the household. One form of archery practice involved blunt, round-headed arrows that were fired at surrounding livestock without the possibility of causing harm. Another game was the cock-shy. Expendable cocks, often those who performed poorly in the fighting pits, were tied by the foot to a stand or tree stump, and archers would take it in turns to fire their arrows into the body of the rooster, continuing long after the unfortunate creature had succumbed to its wounds.

Another version was cock-throwing, in which a group of youngsters would catch a cockerel, tie it to the ground or bury it up to its neck, and throw sticks and stones at it until it was dead. The game was usually a highlight of Shrove Tuesday celebrations. From this rural version developed a more "gentlemanly" form.

Cock-shying, as illustrated in Joseph Strutt's *Sports and Pastimes of the People of England* (1801).

The sticks and stones were replaced with "coksteles," specially made weighted sticks. The people of the Basque region of northern Spain also played a game in which a chicken was buried up to its neck, called *oilar jokoa*. Both the bird and the contestants were blindfolded, and, guided by the beat of the *txistulari* (drummer), the players had to locate the creature and remove its head. The game is still played today, most famously in Legazpi in June, but in the modern version it is considered sufficient merely to pat the chicken's head.

The cockerel was a popular target in Britain because of its convenient abundance, but also because of its symbolic association with the French. The birds suffered in a multitude of other ways outside of the cockpits: a sport called "thrashing the hen" (also known as "whip the cock") was popular in England until 1840. Here, a hen was thrown into a sack, which was then strapped to the back of the "hoodman," who also had bells sewn to the hem of his clothes. The other players were blindfolded and given clubs, and had to try to beat the chicken to death as the hoodman evaded them.

"Club and jar" is another example. In a manuscript dated to 1344, preserved by the Bodleian Library, can be found a curious illustration. The drawing shows two figures, one with a hood draped over his eyes and brandishing a large, bulb-ended club, the other standing beside an upturned pot. In his exhaustive study of the history of British entertainments, *The Sports and Pastimes of the People of England* (1801), Joseph Strutt included a copy of the image under the category "Obsolete Pastimes," but knew very little about it. However, if he had only consulted with a German friend, he might have been enlightened as to what lay inside the upside-down pot. For the sport was still played in that country in the 1800s, at fairs and other celebrations, and even survives today in a reduced tradition known as *Hahnenschlag*, which translates roughly as "cock shock" or "cock-beating." Having successfully managed to survive the myriad other forms of torture endured by his kind for man's entertainment, an unfortunate cockerel was caught and trapped beneath a jar. A contestant was then blind-folded and spun until disoriented. He advanced to the approximate position he believed the cock-pot to be and swung wildly at it with his club. Sometimes it would shatter immediately, and sometimes further efforts were required. He was sometimes clued in to the whereabouts of his target by calls from the crowd, but also by the bird itself, which would squawk inside its prison.

The modern version of *Hahnenschlag* does not, of course, incorporate a live rooster. Instead, the contestants are armed with a staff reminiscent of a hockey stick and, guided by the directions of the spectators, attempt to take as few steps as possible to the guessed position (the players are ranked by their number of paces). They then raise the stick high over their heads and bring it down to smash the flowerpot that they are sure is—but often is not—at their feet.

CODEBALL

Popular in 1930s America, codeball was advertised as "the modern and fascinating All-American kicking game . . . healthful enjoyment for golf widows and orphans." It was a combination of golf and soccer, and took its name not from any cryptographic element, as one might assume, but from its inventor, Dr. William Edward Code of Chicago, who created it in 1929. Code came up with the idea at the behest of his friend, Anton Cermak, who was serving on the Cook County Board of Commissioners and wanted to find a game that could be staged in playgrounds, was easy to play, and, most important, was cheap.

The game was played on a fairway with fourteen bowls serving as the holes. A rubber ball six inches in diameter was "teed off" with a kick from the starting point, and from where it landed was kicked again, the goal being to "hole" the ball with as few kicks as possible. It was simple, and required little practice to play competently—perhaps a factor in its short shelf life, for there was very little challenge.

Code managed to get the game recognized by the Amateur Athletic Association and set up the Codeball Company of America to promote the sport, which gave its address as 11 South La Salle Street, Chicago. The CCA advertised in various golfing publications, announcing their "revenue-getter for golf clubs." They claimed to have installed codeball sets at golf courses in Indiana, Idaho, Illinois, Ohio, and Kentucky, and urged interested and forward-thinking course managers to write for details. The game did find a fan base for a few years at least—and the first Codeball Championship was held at Forest Park in St. Louis, Missouri, in 1935. The winner was Bert Gates, who scored 69 for fifteen bowls. As a more appealing alternative to soccer and golf, though, it failed, and Code moved on to develop a fusion of handball and soccer in which the players bounced the ball off walls instead of into holes. He named it "codeball-on-the-court" to avoid confusion, but like its older sibling it fell out of vogue before it could graduate from its trial period.

COMPETITIVE TRUMPET-BLOWING

On the opening day of the Ninety-Sixth Olympiad, held in 396 BC, only one event took place: the trumpets and heralds competition, a new addition to a program that included boxing, wrestling, and racing events. The contest was official recognition of the work of the *kerykes* (heralds) and *salpinktai* (trumpeters) who played a crucial role in announcing the beginning of each event and, afterwards, the names of the victors. Strictly speaking, the contest was not a sport, yet was fought as competitively as any other trial. The trumpeters performed from a special platform near the entrance to the stadium while the judges moved around the auditorium, assessing the clarity and volume of the sound produced. The winners were presented with an olive wreath and honored by having their names included in the official list of Olympic victors, and by being selected as the official trumpeter and herald of that year's ceremony. At the Ninety-Sixth Games, the winning trumpeter was Timaios of Elis; and we have records of further victors, including the remarkable trumpeter Diogenes of Ephesus, who won the Olympic event five times between AD 69 and 85 and was twice hailed *periodonikes*, a title earned by taking gold in the circuit of Olympian, Pythian, Nemean, and Isthmian Games. In total, Diogenes is said to have won eighty trumpet-playing contests.

Another extraordinary competitive trumpet blower was Herodorus of Megara, who served King Demetrius Poliorcetes. Herodorus was a short, muscular man with turbines for lungs—his legendarily powerful trumpet blast won him the Olympic contest a staggering ten times between 328 and 292 BC, and the title *periodonikes* at least seven times. Such was his lung capacity that he was able to blow two trumpets simultaneously, producing a deafening sound that reputedly inspired Poliorketes's army into launching a successful assault on the town of Argos. When training for the competitions, Herodorus had a strict regime: he slept only on the skins of lions and adhered to a daily diet of 6 kilos of wheaten bread, 9 kilos of meat, and 6 liters of wine.

COPSOLE-PULLING

This was a rural British form of tug-of-war, related to the Welsh game *tynnu* (tugging) and the Scottish *sweir-trees* (also known as *sweir-erse* or *sweir-drauchts*), and was a simple but entertaining way for men to prove their strength after some heavy drinking.

Two opponents sat opposite each other on the ground with the soles of their feet pressed against each other. A length of wood, such as the neck yoke of a horse-drawn carriage, was then placed between the men, who each grabbed hold of one end. The match would start, and they would both wrench the timber in their direction. The moment one player was lifted from his seat into the air, his opponent had won. *Sweir-trees* was played in much the same way, but with the contestants holding hands.

In the history of almost every culture in the world there was played a tugging match of one kind or another (see the sport of Viking skin-pulling, for example). In Japan, an alternative tugging game was played, called *kubi-hiki*. Just as with copsole-pulling, two opponents sat opposite each other (here cross-legged), but in place of a wooden block a sash was twisted or tied into a figure-eight shape, and a loop was placed over each man's head to hang around his neck. They then fought to pull each other forward so that one man ended up face-first in the other's lap.

CRICKET ON HORSEBACK

In the *Kentish Gazette* of April 29, 1794, there appeared the following puzzling advertisement:

> Cricketing on Horseback. A very singular game of cricket will be played on Tuesday, the 6th of May in Linsted Park, between the Gentlemen of the Hill and the Gentlemen of the Dale, for one guinea a man. The whole to be performed on horseback. To begin at nine o'clock, and the game to be played out. A good ordinary on the ground by John Hogben.

To this day the notice is a mystery, for there are no surviving records as to how the match was played, the result, or if it even took place at all. One might assume this to be a unique experiment, but according to Joseph Strutt, a mention of a separate staging of this bizarre sport is made in Lillywhite's *Score Sheets*, which states that in 1800 Sir Horace Mann organized a cricket match to be played on ponies in Harrietsham, Kent.

Various theories as to how the game might have been played have been suggested over the years, including the use of a specially made elongated bat and balls the size of soccer balls for ease of hitting. Modern re-creations have even been attempted. But while the mystery is an enjoyable brain-teaser, the most likely explanation is that the name "cricket on horseback" is an early alternative name for equestrian polo. As the British encountered the game in India, those witnessing the sport for the first time naturally attempted to relate what they were seeing to what was already familiar. A little investigation finds a useful article in the nineteenth-century publication *Thornton's Gazetter*, in which the term "cricket on horseback" is used by the English writer to describe the favorite pastime of the Botis of Ladakh—namely, polo. There were other confusing misnomers, too: a writer of the same period named Godfrey Vigne was also determined to form his own label for the sport, referring to it as "hockey on horseback."

DONKEY-BOXING

The biannual Palio di Siena is an Italian horse racing event that dates back to the fourteenth century, when the various *contrade* (wards) of the city competed against each other in a violent series of racing, jousting, and brawling events. This was a time when sports were essentially a form of military training; and so, in some respects, the brutality that to modern eyes seems gratuitous and depraved was not just necessary preparation for the horrors of medieval battle but no doubt a product of them, too. The *asinate a pugna* event, or donkey-boxing, which was most popular in the sixteenth century, is a good example of this.

Asinate a pugna was a combination of donkey racing and mass fistfighting that took place in the main piazza. Each *contrade* submitted a team of up to thirty *pugillatori* (fighters) who entered the square led by their *capitani* and bearing the banner of their district. Each team also brought with them an ass, which was painted from head to hoof in the team's colors, matching the doublets, caps, and hose of the men. Weapons were forbidden: staves and whips were confiscated, and all rings were removed from fingers. Any flouters of this rule were fined fifty *scudi* in gold. The teams paraded around the Piazza del Campo until it was time to begin. The fighters fixed their flags in the ground, and the spectators and any other noncombatants left the arena to settle into their vantage points, leaving the circular track clear. The donkeys were then led to the starting line, and the fighters took their places around the animals.

The signal was then given to start the race, which was when all hell broke loose. The *pugillatori*, of whom there were hundreds in number, threw themselves at both the rival donkeys and the men attempting to mount and ride them to the finish line. The creatures were punched, kicked, bitten, wrenched in every direction, and wrestled to the ground; anything to prevent them from completing a circuit. The crowd yelled, hissed, and applauded as the men rained blows upon the donkeys and each other; rarely was a man able to straddle the ass for more than a second before he was hauled off the saddle and swallowed up by the mob. Sometimes a team of *pugillatori* even managed to bodily lift both ass and rider into the air and carry them out of the stadium, leaving the pair unable to rejoin the race unless they reentered at the exact same spot they left, something the donkey was in no particular rush to do. The victors were the animal and rider who managed to force their way through the throng to complete two laps of the circuit, winning for their *contrade* forty *scudi*, and an extra twenty to be distributed among the players. The men are described as being left in a terribly bloody state by the event, and so the condition of the donkeys is too horrible to imagine, especially when taking into consideration the fact that the game would last for more than an hour.

DUCK-BAITING

Duck-baiting, or ducking, was one of the favorite pastimes of British pub drinkers in the pre–Industrial Revolution era; in fact, it is largely forgotten that the common pub name "Dog and Duck" owes its origin as much to this practice as to duck hunting. In this case, the arena for the baiting was usually a nearby pond or piece of open water owned by the pub landlord, who would take bets and offer a discounted entry fee to those who brought dogs with them, for they held the status of patron of an activity referred to by *The Gentleman's Magazine* of 1816 as a "polite and humane sport."

The most famous of these ducking ponds was that of Mr. John Ball, whose establishment, the Salutation, was located in the area now known as Balls Pond Road. Ball also hosted bear-baitings and other savageries at his public house, and was such a popular

"The canine fanciers trying the qualities of their Dogs at a Duck Hunt," another illustration by Theodore Lane from the 1830s. Pubs called the Dog and Duck often have a surprising heritage.

figure in the seventeenth century that he was commemorated on a coin circulated locally at the time.* The last surviving duck-baiting site was fifty yards from Bond Street, remembered by the naming of Ducking Pond Mews.

A duck with its wings pinioned was released into the pond, and a spaniel was sent in after it. Unable to fly, the bird was forced to speed around the water or dive beneath the surface in order to escape. Of course, there was very little chance of it doing so. After finally growing weary from the pursuit, the duck would succumb to the dog, who killed it and brought it ashore.

A drinking hole on Hertford Street in London was as notorious for its ducking as it was for its generosity with Right Lincoln

---

* Until 1672, all coinage produced by the crown was made of gold and silver, and so, for those in need of change, leaden tokens were produced by companies, tradesmen, and even private individuals for limited local circulation.

Ale for those attending the event. An advertisement of a baiting from 1748 survives, and gives a sense of the jovial nature of the affair:

> June 25, 1748—At May Fair Ducking Pond, on Monday next, the 27th inst., Mr. Hooton's Dog Nero, (ten years old, with hardly a tooth in his head to hold a duck, but well known for his goodness to all that have seen him hunt,) hunts six ducks for a guinea, against the bitch called the Flying Spaniel, from the Ducking Pond on the other side of the water, who has beat all she has hunted against, except Mr. Hooton's Good-Blood. To begin at two o'clock
> . . . Note. Right Lincoln Ale.

One alternative form of the sport disregarded the participation of dogs in favor of tying a live owl to the duck's back. The duo were launched into the water, and the owl's screeching protestations would startle the duck, prompting it to dive. When it resurfaced the spectacle would be repeated until the duck had drowned its passenger.

Like many of the baiting sports, ducking appealed to those of every social class, and was supposedly a favorite of Charles II and many of his prime nobility. Its demise is attributed to London's urban development and subsequent scarcity of ponds rather than any increase in concern for the ducks' welfare.

DWILE FLONKING

In mid-1960s Norfolk, it became a favorite activity of locals to gather in a large group, dance to an accordion, and hit each other in the face with beer-soaked rags. The sport was known as dwile flonking, and, while chaotic, possessed its own set of rules—although these were often described as confusing, especially as the game progressed and buckets of alcohol were downed. They also varied considerably depending on the venue and levels of inebriation, but essentially were as follows.

Two teams of twelve players were selected to take part and dress in a traditional costume that consisted of a porkpie hat, a collarless shirt, "lijahs" (trousers tied with string at the knee), hobnail boots, and a straw or clay pipe (smoking optional). A "dull-witted person" was then selected to act as referee, or "jobanowl," and a sugar beet was tossed to decide which team should start. The game would begin when the jobanowl cried, "Here y'go t'gither!"

The flonking team nominated a member of their rank to be the flonker. He or she was then encircled by the nonflonking team, who joined hands (in the style of the hokey pokey) and danced—to music provided by accordionists of varying ability—in a circle around the flonker. This was known as "girting." The flonker, meanwhile, who was sometimes blindfolded, was armed with a "driveler"—usually a broom handle with a rag attached to the tip. He then dipped his driveler into a mop bucket filled with beer and slowly turned in the opposite direction to the girters. When the music stopped, he lashed out at the nearest player with his driveller in an attempt to flonk him and score points.

The points system was always disputed, but was usually scored

87

thusly: a direct hit to the face secured the flonker a "wonton" (three points); a sloppy blow to the upper body was a "morther" (two points); and catching a girter between the knee and waist won you a "ripper" (one point). Each flonker was allowed two attempts each turn, but if all he scored were two "swadgers," or misses, then he was deemed to have fouled and was forced to "take the pot," which meant downing a large quantity of beer from the "gazunder" (chamberpot) while the girters sang "The Dwile Flonkers Lament." Anyone who was sober at the end of the game also lost a point.

The girters would then take their turn, called a "snurd," with a full game featuring four such changeovers. Through all this, the role of the jobanowl was to keep the game interesting by varying the speed and direction of the rotating dancers and heavily penalizing any player not taking the game seriously.

After hours of excessive drinking and slaps in the face with beery cloths, the trophy was finally awarded to the visibly unsteady victors. This was the gazunder, an ornate pewter chamberpot. For the annual championships held in Beccles and Bungay in the 1960s and '70s, a specially made gazunder was donated by Adnams Brewery.

The origin of the sport is disputed. Some say it dates back to the sixteenth century: "dwile" is thought to derive from the Dutch word *dweil*, meaning floor cloth, possibly introduced by Flemish weavers during the Middle Ages. The origins of "flonk" are a little vaguer, though. It could perhaps be based on "flong," an old past tense of "fling"; others argue that flonk is an old English ale; or possibly it could be derived from "flong," a printing term referring to a paper mold. However, following the Beccles fête of 1966, the

Eastern Daily Press caused turmoil when it ran an article questioning the official history of dwile flonking, claiming the county archivist had been unable to find any previous reference to the game in the county records. It is thought that the sport was in fact an invention of a group of apprentice printers who met weekly at the Norwich technical college. They claimed to have discovered the game in a book entitled *Waveney Rules of 1585* that they found in an attic, but it is now believed they created the game themselves as a publicity stunt for the 1966 Beccles village fête. "We used to sit down during lunch breaks in between rows of type cases and discuss amendments to the rules," recalled one of the inventors, Graham Roberts. In fact, dwile flonking can be traced back a little further, to a comedy sketch featured in Michael Bentine's show *It's a Square World*, broadcast in the early 1960s.

The rural sport was again in the spotlight in 1967 when the Three Tuns pub in Bungay applied for a special license permitting a gathering of the Waveney Valley Dwile Flonking Association. The magistrate inquired as to the nature of the sport, and the applicants and other members of the court had to admit they did not know. It was left to a member of the public in the gallery to explain with an impromptu demonstration. In a brief moment of fame, the Waveney Valley Dwile Flonkers were invited to appear on *The Eamonn Andrews Show* in 1967. Dwile flonking hit the headlines and prompted letters from sports enthusiasts across the world requesting a dwile flonking rule book.

In 2010, in an attempt to revive interest in the sport, the inaugural Dwile Flonking World Championships were planned to be held at the Dog Inn pub, in Ludham, Great Yarmouth. Unfortunately, word of the event reached the Norfolk District Council,

A flonker with his driveler in the Waveney Valley Dwile
Flonking Association, 1967. (*Alamy*)

who decided that it contravened recently instituted speed drinking laws, and the sport was banned.

EEL-PULLING

It was raining stones," wrote *De Amsterdammer* journalist Johan Geerke in July 1886, reporting from the midst of one of the bloodiest riots in Amsterdam's history. "A walk through the Boomstraat and the Lindenstraat and behind the crowds showed us that the stones used as projectiles were prepared by boys, who tore them up out of the streets and broke them into the pieces with a variety of instruments, and then brought them to the barricades in baskets."

Three days before, tensions between the working-class residents of Jordaan and their bourgeois neighbors had reached a breaking point. Unemployment was at an all-time high, the long winter had been particularly cruel, and overall despair was widespread. The annual July *kermis* (fairs) were the only opportunities for the people to forget the troubles heaped upon them.

On the afternoon of Sunday, July 25, 1886, one such festival was under way, and the district was celebrating with cock-throwing, sack races, and other events. In an effort to keep the party atmosphere alive, someone suggested staging a *palingtrekken* (eel-pulling). This was a medieval sport popular at fairs and festivals across Europe and a particular favorite of the Dutch, despite the fact that the authorities had banned the activity years before, condemning it as "a cruel popular entertainment."

A rope was strung across a waterway, to the center of which was fixed a live eel chosen for its size and lubricity; the fish was also usually greased with soap to offer more of a challenge. As it dangled high over the canal, competitors in their boats would take turns passing under the creature and leaping into the air to try to pull it free. The person who managed to come away with the eel (or, more accurately, part of the eel) was declared the winner and could cook his prize for dinner. For spectators, the fun came from watching the contestants lose their balance and tumble into the water.

Crowds formed along the Lindengracht canal to watch the competition and place bets. The rope was tied across the water, and the plumpest, oiliest eel was bought from a local vendor and hooked into place. The eel-pullers had managed two attempts at seizing the fish when a passing policeman noticed the *palingtrekken* in progress. He tore down the rope and ordered the crowd to disperse. For the people of Jordaan, this was the final straw.

An eel-pulling, or *palingtrekken*, as shown on the cover of
L'Illustration, August 7, 1886, just after the riots in Amsterdam.

The man was struck with an umbrella and thrown down a flight
of stairs. More policemen quickly arrived, but found themselves
beaten back by a bombardment of bricks and stones.

The situation quickly escalated into a full-scale riot, and when
the mob was joined by a nearby group of socialist protesters, further violence broke out. Cobblestones were ripped up and used
to form missiles and makeshift barricades in the Lindenstraat
and the Boomstraat. After three days of intermittent fighting,
the army was finally called in, with bloody consequences. The
troops responded to the stone-throwing by opening fire. In the
brief ensuing mêlée, twenty-six civilians lost their lives, some of

whom were indoors hiding from the fighting; a further 136 were wounded.

Rather amazingly, the eel that had been at the center of the *Palingoproer* (Eel Riot) turned up years later at auction, in February 1913. Lot 1324, offered by the auction house Bom in the Warmoesstraat, was a dry brown husk, accompanied by a certificate of authenticity assuring the purchaser that this was indeed the eel that had sparked the riot, and that "the holes for the rope are still visible." The fish sold for 1¾ guilders to a retired infantry lieutenant, who disappeared before anyone could ask what he intended to do with it.

"Goose riding" (also known as "gander-pulling" and "gooseneck tearing") was a similar sport that was also popularly played across Europe at about this time. A live goose was strung up by its feet to a pole or length of rope tied between two posts. The competitors rode horses at speed underneath, attempting to wrench the bird's head free; doing so would win them the body. A gruesome account from a French source suggests the pullers may even have bitten the head off, as the winner was described as needing "strong jaws and good teeth."

FIERY KITES

One book in particular is credited with inspiring a young Sir Isaac Newton to take up a life of scientific endeavor. Published in 1634, John Bate's *The Mysteryes of Nature and Art* is a beautifully illustrated technical compendium of inventions, models, and practical guides divided into four sections: "Water workes," "Fyer workes," "Drawing, Colouring, Painting, and Engraving," and "Divers Experiments." The section on fireworks is particularly striking and features instructions on how to make your own "flying Dragons," "fire wheels," "compounded rockets," and the rather disconcerting "rayning fire." The most vividly illustrated entry, though, is that of the "fire Drakes." These were a type of large kite to which were attached great streaming tails of firecrackers, lanterns, and other pyrotechnics, and were especially popular with those who enjoyed terrifying proximate members of the public. This included a young Isaac Newton, who, according to his friend William Stukeley, "invented the trick of a paper lanthorn with a candle in it, ty'd to the tail of a kite. This wonderfully affrighted all the neighbouring inhabitants for some time, & caus'd not a little discourse on market days, among the country people, when over thir mugs of ale."

Here are Bate's original instructions for how to make fire drakes, should you wish to engage in the rather exciting prospect of reviving Isaac Newton's favorite sport:

You must take a peece of linnen cloth of a yard or more in length; it must bee cut after the forme of a pane of glasse; fasten two light stickes crosse the same, to make it stand at breadth; then smeare it over with linseed oyle, and liquid varnish tempered together, or else wet it with oyle of peter, and unto the longest corner fasten a match prepared with salpeter water (as I have taught before) upon which you may fasten divers crackers, or Saucissons; betwixt every of which, binde a knot of paper shavings, which will make it flye the better; within a quarter of a yard of the cloth, let there bee bound a peece of prepared stoupell [match], the one end whereof, let touch the cloth, and the other enter into the end of a Saucisson: then tie a small rope of length sufficient to rayse it unto what heighth you shall desire, and to guide it withall: then fire the match, and rayse it against the winde in an open field; and as the match burneth, it will fire the crackers, and saucissons, which will give blowes in the ayre; and when the fire is once come unto the stoupell, that will fire the cloth, which will shew very strangely and fearefully.

John Bate's impression of flying a fiery kite, an idea that was taken up by Isaac Newton.

FIREWORK BOXING

In 1825 a young boy working at Brock's Fireworks factory in Baker's Row, Whitechapel, accidentally sparked a firecracker. In a panic he tossed it into a barrel and ran. The barrel was filled with gunpowder. The ensuing explosion shook houses and smashed windows within a two-mile radius. Brock's, founded in 1698 and England's oldest fireworks company, moved to south London and soon struck a deal with the Crystal Palace to provide free public firework displays that came to be known as "Brock's Benefits."

The shows were constructed on an extravagant scale. Large frames of catherine wheels, sparklers, and other illuminations played backing to symphonic rocketry and unique displays of pyrotechnic innovation. The crowd favorite was Brock's patented invention: the 'Living Fireworks.' These were scenes in which fireworks would come to life in the shape of moving characters, including groups of dancers performing the "Sailor's Hornpipe" and *Salome*, cats fighting, cockfights, a boxing kangaroo in 1893, a Noah's Ark procession with elephants spraying sparks from their trunks, and boxing men. The crowds were captivated, and Brock's shows entertained dignitaries such as the Shah of Persia, Naser al-Din (who was particularly amused by the "fighting cocks" display), and the Emperor of Germany, for whom the boxing men display "caused unbounded delight" in 1892, according to *Strand Magazine*.

The boxing men was Brock's signature "living display," and for a while it was a mystery as to how the effect was achieved, with some suspecting the use of complex automata. But then the secret was uncovered: the blazing pyrotechnics were strapped to live men, or, as the company referred to them, "living actors in fire." The employees dressed in specially commissioned asbestos suits, to which frames of fireworks were attached and lit. The brilliance of the background display obscured the men from being seen by the crowds, and the outlined figures appeared to be stick figures moving and sparring together of their own accord.

Though Brock's Living Fireworks were very much cutting-edge inventions, the idea of "living actors in fire" shares much with the pyrotechnic sport of early English fireworkers, who would often lead processions and pageantry displays. These shows were essentially about creating noise: the men would ignite explosive mixtures in handheld instruments that would crackle and

Two asbestos-clad employees of Brock's Fireworks Ltd. prepare to box with lit fireworks strapped to their bodies. (*Popular Science*, May 1926)

pour out sparks. To protect themselves from the flying sparks, the fireworkers would dress from head to toe in foliage, and were thus known as "Green Men," an association that persisted for centuries. The fireworkers would salute each other with the phrase "Stay green!"—a tradition alive to this day, though barely so.

In fact, the figure of the Green Man has a fascinating story of its own. A pre-Christianity symbol of nature and regrowth, it can be found rooted in the history of cultures all over the world: from architectural motifs adopted by churches incorporating local pagan myths to the naming of many British pubs. An illustration of such a figure can be found in John Bate's *The Mysteryes of Nature and Art*, on the title page of the second book, entitled "Teaching most plainly, and withall most exactly, the composing of all manner of Fire-works for Triumph and Recreation." In fact, there is an even earlier reference: a record of Anne Boleyn's coronation in 1533 states, "At the head of her procession was an enormous fire-breathing dragon followed by a green man casting fire and making a hideous noise."

FLAGPOLE-SITTING

Remarkable from the first to the last was Alvin "Shipwreck" Kelly—a man of patience, poise, and an iron derrière. Kelly, who claimed to have survived a train wreck, two aircraft accidents, three car crashes, and five naval disasters (including the sinking of the *Titanic*, hence the nickname), was a Hollywood stuntman who came to prominence in 1924 through his championing of the sport of flagpole-sitting, which consists of exactly what you think it does. As a result of a bet with a friend (though others say it was a publicity stunt for a department store), Kelly sparked a national craze by perching atop a Philadelphia flagpole for thirteen hours and thirteen minutes. Soon, others were challenging the self-proclaimed "King of the Pole" with stunts of their own, the goal being to last as long as possible and push the record ever further. Finally, Shipwreck determined to reclaim his title with a time that could never be beaten.

In 1930, at the Steel Pier in Atlantic City, New Jersey, Kelly was winched up into position before a crowd of around twenty thousand spectators and began his greatest feat. Despite the tiny perch, he carried out his usual daily routines: eating meals, bath-

Alvin "Shipwreck" Kelly tempts fate on Friday the Thirteenth of October, 1939, by adapting his flagpole-sitting habit and sitting on his head instead. (*Corbis*)

ing himself, reading the paper. When it came time to sleep—the sitting had to be completely uninterrupted for it to be official— Kelly had devised his own trick to minimize the danger of suspending himself unconscious and untethered fifty feet above the ground. He etched holes similar to those of a bowling ball into the sides of the flagpole and inserted his fingers. Should he start to slump in his sleep, the pain of having his fingers tweaked would jolt him awake.

When the Atlantic City stunt came to a close, Kelly had spent 1,177 hours in the air, a little over forty-nine days, far exceeding even his own expectations.* The record stood, for there were few attempts to beat it—interest in the sport nosedived when the Great Depression hit, and, although there was a brief resurgence after World War II headed by Kelly himself, it soon passed. By his own estimation, Kelly spent a career total of 20,613 hours sitting on top of flagpoles in all weather—in fact, he even recorded the variety of the latter, enduring 47 hours of snow, 1,400 hours of rain and sleet, and 210 hours in below-freezing temperatures.

The man and his sport were soon forgotten. "Shipwreck" Kelly died on October 11, 1952, alone and living on welfare. He was found hugging a collection of newspaper articles from his pole-sitting glory days.

---

* As impressive as this achievement is, it pales in comparison to that of St. Simeon Stylites the Elder (ca. 388–459), the Syriac ascetic saint who lived atop a pillar for thirty-seven years.

FLYTING

Flytings were extemporary swearing matches that placed a value on the imagination and verbal dexterity of the participants, who would exchange insults with impressive wordplay in a sense similar to modern rap battles, but with an intensity of vitriol and florid vocabulary that is hard to fully comprehend by modern standards. Flytings are examples of sport in its oldest sense, and can be found in Old Norse and Anglo-Saxon literature such as *Beowulf*, in which they are used as an overture to battle. In *Egil's Saga* (ca. 1200), the Icelandic bard Egill Skallagrímsson unwisely insults Eric Bloodaxe, King of Norway, and his wife, Gunnhild, with "This inheriting traitor [who] disinherits me by betrayal" and "Lawbreaker not lawmaker . . . brother's murderer . . . [whose] guilt stems all from Gunnhild."

It was in medieval Scotland, however, where flyting was most relished; and, as a case study in such contests, *The Flyting of Dunbar and Kennedy* (1503), in which insults fly with a breathtaking abundance of vileness, is considered one of the most famous examples. To Dunbar's opening warning that should he choose to flyte the seas would boil and the moon eclipse as a result, Kennedy launches a retort to "Dirtin Dunbar" in which he uses, among many others, phrases like "fantastick fule" and "wan fukkit funling" ("ill-conceived foundling"). In response, Dunbar labels Kennedy a "Cuntbitten crawdon" ("pox-infected coward"). Kennedy brands Dunbar a "shit but wit" who would "like to throw shit by the cartload" (one of the earliest uses of shit as an insult). Impressive alliteration is then incorporated in a furious salvo against Dunbar: "Deuill dampnit dog, sodomyte insatiable . . .

A depiction of Norse gods assembled as in the *Poetic Edda*
poem *Lokasenna* by Lorenz Frølich, 1895.

Thy commissar Quintine biddis the cum kis his ers" ("Your friend
Quintin bids you come and kiss his ass"). The Dunbar-Kennedy
spat also contains the first examples of several other swear words
used today, such as *get* (git) in its early meaning of "bastard":
"Fals tratour, feyndis get" ("False traitor, devil's bastard"). In *The
Flyting of Montgomerie and Polwart* (ca. 1585), the invitation is
extended to "kiss the cunte of ane kow," and in *Answer to [the]
King's Flyting* (1535–36), an incensed flyter declares: "Ay fukkand
like ane furious Fornicatour."

By 1600 the popularity of hurling foul language as sport had
wilted in favor of witty and more poetic language, but the tra-
ditions can be detected in confrontations from writings of the

period. Shakespeare is often cited, such as the exchanges between Lear and Kent, but also the following back-and-forth between Katherina and Petruchio in *The Taming of the Shrew*:

> *Katherina*: I knew you at the first,
> You were a moveable [piece of furniture].
> *Petruchio*: Why, what's a moveable?
> *Katherina*: A joint-stool.
> *Petruchio*: Thou hast hit it. Come and sit on me.
> *Katherina*: Asses are made to bear, and so are you.
> *Petruchio*: Women are made to bear, and so are you.

Today, little influence remains of flyting in its true form; the nearest comparisons to be found are the verbal-sparring rap battles known as playing, sounding, or playing the dozens; and perhaps even the modern American tradition of the comedy roast, in which a celebrated figure is subjected to mockery by his friends and colleagues with witty lampooning, with no language considered too foul, a special license of the event that is shared with the original flyting contests.

FOX TOSSING

By the standards of any era, *Fuchsprellen* (fox tossing) was a most bizarre spectacle. Played by both men and women, the aim of the game was to launch the unsuspecting animals into the air as high as possible. This was achieved with a strip of netting or fabric laid across the ground, known as the *Prellgarn* or *Prelltuch* ("bouncing cloth"). Standing twenty to twenty-five feet apart, the tossing partners each took a firm hold of an end of these slings slackened in the middle and waited. The foxes were released from side enclosures into the main area to run terrified around the pitch before stepping onto the sling of a waiting team of tossers. At this, the couple would yank the sling taut and send the fox flying into the air, often as high as twenty-four feet. Part of the fun was watching the animals maneuver in midair as they attempted to land on their paws. The sport may have had its roots in an ancient superstition: to bring good luck in the winter months, a dog or fox, representing the wicked winter spirit, was repeatedly thrown into the air with a blanket until it was dead.

Usually taking place in royal courtyards and gardens, though sometimes practiced in a countryside arena specially formed with canvas screens (see Chasse aux Toiles for other examples of sport in this setting), fox tossing developed from the sport favored by Johann Georg I, Elector of Saxony from 1611 to 1656. The elector was famous for organizing huge animal battles in Dresden's central market in which great Polish aurochs, bears, wolves, stags, and boars were pitted against each other in a bloody battle royal. When the fighting had died down, the elector would courageously step into the arena and dispatch the remaining contestants with a spear.

According to Hans Friedrich von Fleming in his *Der vollkommene teutsche Jäger*, in preparation for a fox tossing match the head gamekeeper would instruct his staff to capture as many live foxes, hares, and vermin as they could manage in the weeks beforehand. The animals would be stored in a specially built stone enclosure, where they were fed and well cared for. When the day arrived, they were rounded up and deposited in a pen beside the fox tossing court. In the event the competition was played in a courtyard, the paved *Schlossplatz* would be prepared with sawdust to cause erratic landings and also reduce the risk of the wretched creature suffering a fractured skull, thereby enabling repeat tossings. The animal had very little chance of evading a tossing, as quite often the enclosure contained large numbers of tossers positioned in as many as three lanes. To the delight of both the competitors and the spectators lining the pitch and watching from palace windows, the species of animal released into the tossing ground was often varied to keep things interesting. Initial waves of foxes would be followed by batches of hares, badgers, and even wildcats—sometimes all at once.

When the tossing had drawn to a close, the competitors would then stalk the battleground, finishing off the wounded with some hearty clubbing. Afterwards hares might be released into the arena, and be chased by any remaining foxes around the feet of the guests, providing extra entertainment.

King Leopold I was a noteworthy fan of the sport, and made a point of opening each March season with a celebratory fox tossing match in the Vienna Prater. A visiting Swedish diplomat named Esaias Pufendorf recorded in his diary in March 1672 how remarkable it was to witness the Holy Roman Emperor and King of Germany "Clubbing the foxes himself and throwing sticks at the foxes once they had been tossed, and he did all this with young boys and court jesters, which I thought was a little far from the gravitas a Kaiser should have."

Unsurprisingly, death tolls at the larger fox tossing matches verged on the cataclysmic. Over the course of 1747, the tossing

Friedrich von Fleming shows how fox tossing was deemed
to be a sport for couples to enjoy together.

activities of Augustus III, Elector of Saxony and King of Poland, resulted in the deaths of 414 foxes, 281 hares, 39 badgers, and one wildcat. This tally, however, paled in comparison to that of a single earlier match organized by his father.

Augustus II (1670–1733), King of Poland, Grand Duke of Lithuania, and vulpicidal maniac, was a man of immense physical strength. He was said to be capable of holding up a fully equipped cavalryman in one outstretched palm, and to possess a fondness for snapping horseshoes with his bare hands. Feats such as these earned him the sobriquets "the Strong," "the Saxon Hercules," and the "Iron-Hand." (He was also rumored to have fathered over three hundred illegitimate children by the age of twenty-seven, although this is thought to be a slight exaggeration.) In particular, the monarch loved to demonstrate his renowned strength at fox tossing matches by employing only a single finger to pull on the tossing sling while it was held at the other end by two of his strongest subjects. The final death toll of one fox tossing match held at his Dresden palace came to a staggering 687 foxes, 533 hares, 34 badgers, and 21 wildcats. As a *pièce de résistance* for his guests, Augustus then had thirty-four young wild boars and three wolves released into the enclosure "to the great delectation of the cavaliers, but to the terror of the noble ladies, among whose hoop-skirts the wild boars committed great havoc."

The sport took on an even more bizarre form when, at the court of Brunswick, masked fox tossing was introduced. The noblemen adopted the garb of heroes, hobgoblins, and other mythical creatures, while the ladies chose the costumes of nymphs, sprites, goddesses, or Muses to participate in the baroque bloodbath. The foxes and hares were "dressed up in bits of cardboard, gaudy cloth, and tinsel," often as caricatures of politicians and other unpopular figures. After the body count had been scored and the viscera wiped away, the guests would be treated to an outdoor play or led on a relaxing candlelit stroll through the grounds.

The sport wasn't entirely without risk for the competitors, however. The chances of being clawed, chewed, and, in some cases, charged were accepted as high, and many participants went away with the souvenir of fresh scar tissue. The wildcats were a particular culprit, with one writer noting that they "do not give a pleasing kind of sport, for if they cannot bury their claws and teeth in the faces or legs of the tossers, they cling to the tossing-slings for dear life, and it is next to impossible to give one of these animals a skillful toss."

THE GAME OF THE BRIDGE
AND OTHER CITY BATTLES

Among its various roles, sport can serve as a release: of tension, of frustration, and of aggression. In no other arena is this truer than that of the medieval Italian "city battle," a collection of events among which the aforementioned donkey-boxing is found. In order to reduce day-to-day violence, the authorities of European cities would stage grand mock battles in which all citizenry could participate to vent their anger and enjoy the thrill of "safe" battle by braining each other with clubs, stones, and even snowballs. In fact, as unlikely as it sounds, mass snowball fights, when done in the medieval style (or, as some might say, done properly), were dangerous affairs in which injury was a common result. They could even be lethal: a document from 1438 records a Dominican friar playing with a youth "with snow for the purpose of recreation." The friar had apparently been struck with one too many snowballs, because he threw one so forcefully in return that the child died of his injuries fifty-two days later. Fearing the people would render each other unfit for military service, officials were quick to stamp out any unauthorized snowball skirmishes. A report from Perugia in 1371 mentions one such subduing and describes how the snowball throwers chose to completely ignore the guards sent to break up the fight with clubs. In Basle, decrees banning snowball fights were repeatedly made between 1378 and 1656.

It wasn't just snow that was thrown in these grand fights. As early as 1306, the city of Bologna played host to the *ludus graticulorium*, in which crowds of people hurled raw eggs at each other, an early forerunner of the modern Spanish tomato-throwing festival, La Tomatina, which takes place in the Valencian town of Buñol. Most dangerous of all was the *battaglia dei sassi* (battle of the stones) held in Perugia and Siena. Organized by the Compagnia del Sasso (Company of Stones), thousands of players took part in a battle that saw the occupants of the northern part of town clash with those of the southern by showering one another with rocks. This was only the first part of the game: after the opening salvos, the men set upon each other with clubs and fists, protected in part by helmets, wooden armor, and shields. Identical to this was the *gioco delle pugna* held in Siena. A critical source from 1425 described the carnage:

> Go on, then! Tomorrow you will see charming bloodshot eyes, fine pale faces, many bandaged arms and legs, as many lacking teeth, let alone internal injuries . . . Two-thirds of the entertainment belongs to the audience, only the rest to the players, and in addition they suffer broken sides, cut foreheads, sprained and broken extremities, ribs, chins . . .

The government frequently opposed these battles, but no one seems to have taken much notice of this. The Sienese diarist Allegro Allegretti referred to the *pugna* as *"un belissimo giucco"* (beautiful game) in 1494, and when Charles V visited the city in 1536 a battle was held in his honor, which he is said to have enjoyed tremendously. One term used to describe these battles was *mazza-scudo* ("club and shield"), and the most famous *mazzascudos* were those staged in Florence—in particular the last one, held in 1582 at the behest of Grand Duke Francis I of Tuscany. He paid eighty-eight *scudos* to have it as part of the wedding celebrations for his daughter, Eleonor de' Medici, who was marrying Vincenzo Gonzaga. Things got a little out of hand, however, and the romantic gift had to be brought to a close early so that the multiple dead and wounded could be dealt with.

Elsewhere in Italy, the *gioco del ponte* (game of the bridge) of Pisa was a *mazzascudo* that continued into the eighteenth century. The game originally started in the traditional manner, with inhabitants of the various sectors of the city attacking each other until one group managed to drive the others from the field. In the

An eighteenth-century print of the *gioco del ponte*, a major event in Pisa.

fifteenth century the battleground shifted to the bridge across the River Arno, and it became a contest for possession of the bridge between the citizens of the north and the south. Armed with a *targone* (an elongated shield that doubled as a club), the armies marched in the bright livery of their district to a barrier in the center of the bridge and traded insults. Then, on a signal from the grand duke, the barrier was removed and the two sides clashed, beating and throwing their opponents from the bridge until the winning side was clear. Prisoners were even released for the day so that they could take part, and after the result was announced the winning area of town was specially illuminated, while the losers were left in darkness. In 1574, Henry III of France attended one such bridge fight thrown in his honor during a visit to Venice, but deemed it "too small to be a real war, and too cruel to be a game."

GOLDFISH-SWALLOWING

Although fish, as a food, has had the reputation of being an exceptional brain builder, I understand that this reputation has been proved false," wrote a gentleman named Harold E. Willmott in a letter to the *New York Times* in 1939, in reference to a recently devised sport that was mainly the preserve of student bodies, because everyone else considered it too stupid to try.

Earlier that year, a young freshman at Harvard University named Lothrop Withington, Jr., had set his sights on the class presidency. In a bid to make a name for himself, and under the advice of friends who must surely have gone on to triumphant careers in public relations, Lothrop went through with a $10 wager to swallow a live goldfish in front of one hundred classmates. To settle his stomach he followed it up with a side order of mashed potato.

Intercollegiate competitive spirit being what it is—even when it comes to gulping down living animals—a gauntlet was felt to have been thrown down. "Just to show that those Harvard guys are sissies," said Frank Pope of Franklin & Marshall College two weeks later, before he threw three goldfish down his gullet. Not one to stand by while his school was slighted, Harvard man Irving M. Clark raised the stakes by swallowing twenty-four. "I could have eaten fifty," he wheezed. He was only just starting to enjoy his title (whatever that may have been) when Gilbert Hollandersky of the University of Pennsylvania threw his hat into the bowl by wolfing twenty-five, dipping them in tomato ketchup and wash-

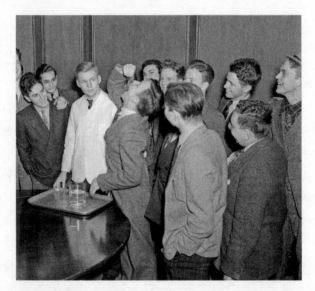

Lothrop Withington, the son of a prominent Boston lawyer, swallows a four-inch goldfish while some of his fellow Harvard students look on. (*Corbis*)

ing them down with orange juice. Despite his efforts, though, the record was smashed by a Boston College student, who in turn was beaten by a freshman at the Mississippi Institute of Technology, all cheerfully ignoring the warnings of doctors that they were exposing themselves to tapeworm infections and anemia.

The students carried on swallowing, driving the record up until it finally stood at 210 fish. There were reports of someone managing 300, but this was unconfirmed, and deemed physiologically impossible. University authorities finally banned the practice amid increasingly urgent health warnings and intensifying public moral dismay, but not before receiving a royal seal of approval from King George VI, who praised the activity during his visit to the United States on the invitation of Franklin Roosevelt in June 1939. Meanwhile, a San Juan Native American named Manuel Archuleta told reporters that the sport was not a recent invention—Native American children had long swallowed goldfish in the belief that it would make them strong swimmers. The students were being ridiculous, he said, whereas the children "had a real reason for swallowing fish."

The craze burnt out quickly, and the newspapers moved on to the next student fad, reporting the story of John Patrick of Chicago University, who ate two whole phonograph records with the declaration: "Fellow students, I did this for alma mater."

THE GREAT TRICYCLE REGATTA

Four venues in New York City have borne the name Madison Square Garden since the first was built in 1879, and in that long and varied history there has perhaps been no stranger event to take place within the Garden's walls than the race staged at five minutes past midnight on October 7, 1888.

"Three strokes will be hit upon a gong," announced the *New York Sun*," and twelve brawny men will start to row around the track . . . There won't be any water and there won't be any boats."

Rowing was hugely popular at the time, and, thanks to substantial media coverage, the heroes of the sport had many followers who had never actually witnessed a race. It had long been a goal of promoters to capitalize on this fan base by somehow bringing the river to the people, a rowing spectacle for those prevented geographically from attending a regatta. The solution had never been found, until the invention of the rowing tricycle, or roadsculler. This was a much cruder device than the rowing machines found in modern gyms: a rickety iron vehicle with one wobbly front wheel and two on the rear that, when worked hard, could reach forward speeds of up to 15 mph.

The plan was quickly put together, and the scale of the peculiarity (as well as a fat prize purse of $10,000) attracted the participation of international rowing champions. There was the Canadian Jacob Gaudaur, the Englishman George Bubear, the American William O'Connor, the Nova Scotia champion John McKay, the local Irish hero John Largan, and a gentleman named Albert Hamm, who was described by one sports reporter as "something of a jolly wanderer, but when he is in good condition he is a hard fellow to beat." The track was 21 feet wide and 220 yards long and was divided into lanes, with the one on the outside reserved for passing, or "spurting." Rowers racing around a modestly sized circuit is a spectacle involving a significant amount of repetition, and therefore one might logically assume the duration of the event would be kept within the confines of an hour or two. However, for reasons known only to the organizers, it was decided that the race would last for *six days*. As it transpired, this was rather optimistic.

Under the glare of electric arc lights and to the fanfare of the 13th Regiment band, the twelve racers yanked themselves into action, and everything went gloriously well for five whole minutes. Fred Plaisted's machine was the first to break down, and then five minutes later William East also suffered mechanical difficulty. They were forced to continue the race on foot until replacement machines could be found. This became such a frequent occurrence in the early stages of the race that the two men whose job it was to lug broken vehicles off the track never left it. Then the first collision happened: John Teemer was thrown from his machine, causing a pileup with racers Ross and Gaudaur. The crowd was delighted, and the city coroner, who was getting ready to leave, retook his seat, remarking: "I guess I'll stay."

The first day of racing ended with Gaudaur in a strong lead, having enjoyed a race free of mishap. The other rowers miserably nursed their bruises and grumbled about the unreliable road-scullers. Nevertheless, the race continued, with more accidents befalling the contestants while Gaudaur continued to enjoy a wide lead. The contest was beginning to wear down the rowers both mentally and physically: Teemer's hands were covered in blisters "as large as copper pennies," and, perhaps in reference to the harsh seat of the rowing tricycle, O'Connor was described as being "crippled elsewhere." There was no respite for the scullers on the third day either. A charcoal fire lit by a food vendor poured thick clouds of smoke onto the track, into which Plaisted and Largan disappeared, eventually emerging with streaming eyes and retching so badly that Largan was forced to temporarily withdraw. After further collisions, breakdowns, and a fistfight between the scullers on the sidelines, Gaudaur went on to win the race, but the affair had been so blighted by calamity that the victory was a hollow one, and the rowers were happy just to be done with it. The event has never been repeated.

HIDDEN HUNTING

In the rare moments he spent outside of the British Museum, the English historian and biographer Thomas Birch (1705–1766) was a keen angler, with a unique approach. He would disguise himself as a tree and stand motionless on riverbanks with his arms outstretched like branches, dangling the line in the water. Wrapped in imitation trunk and blossom, his belief in the costume was such that he claimed any movement on his part would be dismissed by the fish as the effect of a breeze. The terror he caused passersby and the endless teasing he received from his friends eventually persuaded him to hang up the suit, sadly with no mention as to whether he managed to catch anything.*

Hunting in disguise is, of course, as old and as widespread

---

* Fifty years later, the British chemist Sir Humphry Davy (1778–1829), in whose memory a lunar crater is named, dressed daily in an outfit of pure green "so as to resemble vegetable life as closely as it was possible to do." When on countryside shoots he added a large crimson hat to the outfit so as not to be mistaken for scenery, though as one friend pointed out he remained at risk of being shot by an anti-cleric mistaking him for a cardinal.

as the hunt itself, but there are particular occurrences worthy of note. Native American tribes, for example, engaged in "buffalo jumps," a devastating form of trapping dating back over twelve thousand years in which entire herds were destroyed in one fell swoop. Named *pishkun*, which roughly translates to the magnificently evocative "deep blood kettle," a huntsman disguised in buffalo skins crept toward a herd until he had positioned himself between the group and a high cliff edge, in a "driving lane" marked with cairns that led to the precipice. The rest of the men took up their places behind the herd and waited. The explorers Meriwether Lewis and William Clark witnessed a *pishkun* on May 29, 1805, and Clark wrote of what happened next:

> The other indians now surround the herd on the back and flanks and at a signal agreed on all shew themselves at the same time moving forward towards the buffaloe; the disguised indian or decoy has taken care to place himself sufficiently nigh the buffaloe to be noticed by them when they take to flight and runing before them they follow him in full speede to the precepice, the cattle behind driving those in front over and seeing them go do not look or hesitate about following untill the whole are precipitated down the precepice forming one common mass of dead and mangled carcases.

Hundreds of buffalo and other game, such as bison and reindeer, were killed in a single drive, the less fortunate merely immobilized with shattered legs on the rocks below, later to be finished off by their pursuers once they had descended. The deliberate thoroughness of the bovicide was down to the belief that any survivors would pass on their experiences; the animals would collectively learn to be wary of man, and would be harder to hunt in future. The most dangerous role was that of the hunter who served as decoy, for he had to reach the cliff ahead of the animals, swing himself over the edge, and hide in a nook or cranny inside the face before the stampede crushed him. Buffalo jump sites have been found at Head-Smashed-In, Alberta, Canada; Big Goose Creek, Wyoming; Bonfire Shelter, Texas; the Olsen-Chubbuck Bison Kill Site, Colorado; and the Too Close For Comfort site in Montana.

Later, in the forests of medieval Europe, use of the stalking tree was a common ploy, in which canvas screens were painted, decorated with brush, and used as cover by hunters. To bag those animals not to be fooled by approaching shrubbery, a stalking horse was used. This was a live horse draped in fauna, "Some old Jade trained up for that purpose," according to the *Dictionarium Rusticum, Urbanicum & Botanicum* (1717):

[He] will gently, as you would have him, walk up and down in the Water which way you please, plodding and eating the Grass that grows therein; behind whose shoulder, you are to shelter yourself and your gun, bending your Body down low by his side, and keeping his Body still full between you and the Fowl; When you are within shot take your level from before the fore-part of the Horse, giving Fire as it were, between his Neck and the Water, which is much better shooting than under his Belly.

The stalking horse was a favorite of archers, as the docile animal allowed them to get closer to their prey than they had previously managed. It was, however, "frequently inconvenient, and often impracticable," according to Joseph Strutt, and so a stuffed stalking horse became a popular hunting accoutrement. This was made with canvas and filled with straw, light enough to be shifted by the stalker and painted to resemble a lifelike grazing animal. The pole that held it up could be driven into the ground to keep the cover in place. As well as the horse, the hides were also fashioned in the shape of cows, stags, and oxen. The bulkier shape of the cow offered greater coverage, which might have been of particular benefit to one fan of the sport. Henry VIII was an avid stalker; in the inventories of his wardrobes can be found materials used for the frequent making of "stalking coats, and stalking hose for the use of his majesty."

Johann Ridinger illustrates a stalking horse being used to help a hunter shoot wild fowl.

HOPPING

One might assume that the simple act of hopping has limited potential as entertainment for a crowd, but there is a surprisingly far-reaching history to one-legged jumping as a sport. In ancient Greece, youths would play a game called *ascoliasmos*, a battle between contestants to see who could hop for the longest, and at the highest rate. In Britain, one of the earliest examples of one-footed entertainment was the egg dance, which is mentioned in *The Longer Thou Livest, The More Foole Thou Art* (ca. 1568) by William Wager. The Elizabethan play (described by its author as "a very mery and pythie Commedie") contains the lines:

> *Upon my one foote pretely I can hoppe,*
> *And daunce it trimley about an egge.*

As strange as it is to picture, acting like a chicken and dancing around an egg on one foot was a respected custom brought to England by the Saxon gleemen and the Norman minstrels. It was practiced mainly by female dancers, whom Geoffrey Chaucer labels "hoppesteres." As early medieval English society evolved, the style was retained by dancers (though the term "hop" became a pejorative for inferior dancing displays). The egg dance was popular into the eighteenth century, and was even performed at Sadler's Wells in 1770, where the writer Joseph Strutt was among the audience:

> I saw it exhibited, not by simply hopping round a single egg, but in a manner that much increased the difficulty. A number of eggs, I do not precisely recollect how many, but I believe about

twelve or fourteen, were placed at certain distances marked upon the stage; the dancer, taking his stand, was blind-folded, and a hornpipe being played in the orchestra, he went through all the paces and figures of the dance, passing backwards and forwards between the eggs without touching one of them.

Hopping was also an athletic event. In the sixteenth century men raced with one leg at fairs, usually for a ring or other piece of jewelry, which is mentioned by the epigrammatist John Heywood in his *Proverbs* of 1566:

Where wooers hoppe in and out, long time may bring
Him that hoppeth best at last to have the ring—
—I hoppyng without for a ringe of a rushe.

But perhaps the most famous hopping event took place centuries later in 1826, when a renowned runner named William Jackson hopped against a Devonshire man named Richard Roberts. At the Rising Sun drinking hole on Windmill Street in London, the men made a bet of £30 as to who could cover the greatest distance with fifty hops. The race took place on Friday, October 6, on Clapham Common, by the Windmill pub. The two men took their places just before five o'clock and discussed their choice of ground—Jackson wanted to hop along the rough turnpike road, but Roberts objected, as he was racing with bare feet, and so a strip of the grassy common was chosen. Jackson won the toss and immediately stripped down to a pair of small cotton undergarments. He took his run-up to the starting post and then "bounded off with the elasticity of a doe," as one onlooker put it.

Theodore Lane's "The Hopping Match, on Clapham Common. Jackson the runner exhibiting his agility." Nowadays, most people just go jogging there.

He covered the first forty yards in ten hops, gradually weakening until his fiftieth leap carried him to a total distance of 160 yards. Roberts took his turn in a greater state of dress, removing only his shoes, coat, and waistcoat, and launched into his hopping. It became quickly apparent, though, that he was in much worse shape, and he collapsed out of breath and ten yards short. He congratulated Jackson on his victory, only then mentioning that his performance may have been hampered by the fact that he had been bedridden for the previous five days.

HOT COCKLES

Hot cockles dates back to the mid-sixteenth century. Though usually a simple children's game, it was popular with groups of mixed adults, as the tactility offered a racy opportunity for flirtation. Originally a French pastime called *"hautes coquilles,"* the game revolved around a seated female player. A male participant knelt before her and placed his hands behind his back and his head in her lap, so that he was effectively blindfolded by her dress. The other players gathered behind him, and when he cried "Hot cockles, hot!" they would take it in turns to smack his hand or kick him up the backside. He then had to guess the identity of his attacker. If he was correct, he was free. If not, he was struck again.

A depiction of the game entitled *A Game of Hot Cockles* was painted ca. 1660 by Hieronymus Janssens and sits in the Louvre, while a work of Jean-Honoré Fragonard with the same title, painted ca. 1775–80, can be found in the National Gallery of Art in Washington, DC.

123. Hot-Cockles.

Joseph Strutt's illustration of hot cockles in *Sports and Pastimes of the People of England* (1801).

HOT HASTY PUDDING-EATING, JINGLING, AND OTHER SPORTS OF THE FAIR

Fath'r and I went down to camp
Along with Captain Goodin'
And there we saw the men and boys
As thick as hasty puddin.

Yankee Doodle

Hasty pudding is a viscous dish of boiled milk and oats originating from the Middle Ages which was cheap, easy to make, and took very little time to cook—or, as the playwright Thomas Heywood put it in *The English Traveller* (1633): "Longer in eating than it was in making." No doubt this was also behind its selection as the foodstuff of choice in early speed-eating competitions at rural fairs from the seventeenth to the nineteenth centuries. These events were frequented by all kinds of colorful characters (Wordsworth described the Bartholomew Fair as "a Parliament of Monsters" in 1802), and various sports were played, with hot hasty pudding–eating being one such event. The goal was to wolf down as much of the thick and scaldingly hot dish in the shortest amount of time, "so that he whose throat is widest and most callous is sure to be the conqueror," wrote Joseph Strutt in 1801.

The pudding was prepared in an iron pot heated to the highest temperature possible before being poured into basins in front of each of the three competitors. The signal to start was then given, and the competitors scooped the boiling pudding into their mouths with their bare hands (the use of cutlery was forbidden). Techniques varied: some ducked their heads directly into the bowl, but this was usually tried only once. In true Aesopian fashion, the hasty pudding eater who took the time to blow on his bowl would initially fall behind, but often end up triumphing over his opponents, who were struggling to swallow with burnt throats.

"It was, after all, a painful exhibition," wrote the publisher Arthur Hall in 1861, "and, though I laughed as heartily as any of my companions, I was glad to get away, and look at something else unaccompanied by torture."

Here is an old recipe "to make a flour hasty-pudding," taken from *The Art of Cookery Made Plain and Easy* (1747) by Hannah Glasse, should you wish to get a taste of the action yourself:

Take a quart of milk, and four bay-leaves, set it on the fire to boil, beat up the yolks of two eggs, and stir in a little salt. Take two or three spoonfuls of milk, and beat up with your eggs, and stir in your milk, then, with a wooden spoon in one hand, and the flour in the other, stir it in till it is of a good thickness, but not too thick. Let it boil, and keep it stirring, then pour it into a dish, and stick pieces of butter here and there. You may omit the egg if you don't like it; but it is a great addition to the pudding, and a little piece of butter stirred in the milk makes it eat short and fine. Take out the bay-leaves before you put in the flour.

Other diversions at the fairs included competitive smoking, whistling matches, gurning contests, and a game known as "the jingling match." A large roped-off circle was set up, into which entered the players, usually numbering around ten. All but one of them were blindfolded with handkerchiefs, with the one left nominated the jingler. He was given a bell to ring incessantly, and smaller bells were often attached to his clothes and shows. It was his job to run around within the roped boundaries ringing the bell and evading the blindfolded players, who were offered a prize if they managed to grab hold of him. If they failed to catch him, however, the jingler claimed the prize. The match usually lasted between twenty and thirty minutes, and was a favorite with spectators.

As well as recording conversational vernacular, in compiling his *A Classical Dictionary of the Vulgar Tongue* (1785), Francis Grose also mentions other popular fair games, such as tuprunning: "A rural sport practised at wakes and fairs in Derbyshire; a ram, whose tail is well soaped and greased, is turned out to the multitude; any one that can take him by the tail, and hold him fast, is to have him for his own." Another he describes, "mumbling a sparrow," was also a big draw for fair-goers and, though smaller in scale, was equally cruel:

> Mumbling a sparrow; a cruel sport frequently practised at wakes and fairs: for a small premium, a booby having his hands tied behind him, has the wing of a cock sparrow put into his mouth: with this hold, without any other assistance than the motion of his lips, he is to get the sparrow's head into his mouth: on attempting to do it, the bird defends itself surprisingly, frequently pecking the mumbler till his lips are covered with blood, and he is obliged to desist: to prevent the bird from getting away, he is fastened by a string to a button of the booby's coat.

HUMAN-FISHING

There is perhaps no other country where the love of sport is ingrained more firmly into the national character than Australia. It is a nation rich in competitive gaming history, whether it be the Marn Grook ball games and other ancient traditional recreations of the Indigenous Australians; the sports brought by European settlers like cricket; or domestic innovations such as trugo, sphairee, and touch football, among others.

In 1899 there appeared a new sport, reports of which by the Australian press inspired a brief craze (and I do mean brief, for reasons that will become clear). Human-fishing, a physically demanding activity, was described by the New South Wales *Newcastle Herald* as "a rough-and-ready sort of amusement" which appealed to Australians looking to take on a tough new challenge.

The game was played on coasts, rivers, and lakes, and possessed a simplicity that only added to the bizarreness of the spectacle. A strong swimmer assumed the role of the "fish" while his opponent, the "angler," stood on shore. The swimmer was fitted with a harness similar to that of a parachutist, which slid over the shoulders and fastened at the back. The angler was equipped with a rod and strong fishing line, which was unspooled and attached to the swimmer's harness. The swimmer then dived out to the end of the line, and the angler had ten minutes to try to reel in the "fish," who was allowed to do everything possible to prevent this, including breaking the line with his teeth (the use of any tool was forbidden). Victory almost always went to the fish.

The reasons why human-fishing was only briefly experimented

with are surely obvious even to those who might enjoy a good garrotting/drowning. Though it certainly presents an enjoyable picture, however much fun that was had was unfortunately not enough to outweigh the significant dangers, and the game sank like a stone.

HUNTING WITH CHEETAHS

Hunting game with trained big cats can be traced back to the ancient Egyptians, who kept tamed cheetahs as pets. Their usefulness as hunting companions was adopted by the Persians, and the practice spread to India, where it eventually came to the attention of the British. Genghis Khan and Charlemagne both kept hunting cheetahs; Akbar the Great, ruler of the Mughal empire from 1556 to 1605, possessed a menagerie in which as many as a thousand cheetahs were said to be housed. The Crusaders to the Holy Land were also noted to have developed a taste for the sport; and George III was presented with a hunting cheetah by the governor of Madras, a transaction immortalized by George Stubbs in his painting *Cheetah and Stag with Two Indians* (ca. 1765). In historical documents, the distinction between leopards and cheetahs is often blurred; indeed, both were easily tamed and trained for the purpose of the chase. Emperor Leopold I was a particular fan of hunting with leopards; he had been gifted two by a sultan and took them out regularly, until they were slaughtered in 1704, along with every other animal in the imperial menagerie outside Vienna, when the Hungarian rebel Count Károlyi sacked the area with four thousand men.

"Hunting with Trained Leopards," designed by Bruges-
born Joannes Stradanus, engraved by Dutchman
Philip Galle in the early seventeenth century.

The techniques of taming and training the animals for the hunt
changed very little from those used by the ancient Egyptians (and
has been explored in some manner in Cheetah Greyhound Racing). The animals were kept covered with a leather hood, which
was removed only when the trainer provided morsels of meat.
In this way, trust was quickly built, and the cats could be relied
upon to return. They were fitted with collars and each given their
own cart and pair of attendants. Though phenomenal hunters,
they had a tendency to lose interest in their prey if they were not
immediately successful. For this reason, they were kept hooded in
their cages until the quarry was spotted, at which point they were
wheeled in as close as possible and released.

An observer for *The Young Gentleman's Book* of 1832 wrote:

It is most interesting to see their vacant and roving gaze catch and rivet itself upon their victim. An intense singleness of purpose seems to speak in every muscle as the leopard strains upon the rope till it is slipped and he springs down . . . They show training by singling out bucks, for which they get a haunch—whereas they only receive the liver of a doe. It is by forcing this perquisite into their mouth that they are disengaged from the deer.

HUNTING YE OTTER

I am, Sir, a Brother of the Angle, and therefore an enemy of the Otter;
for I hate them so perfectly, because they love fish so well.
Izaak Walton, *The Compleat Angler* (1653)

For a thousand years the otter was persecuted with a passion, thanks to its reputation as a fish-killing scourge. The "cruel tyrant," "midnight pillager," or "sly goose-footed prowler," to give a few of its labels, was hunted relentlessly. "Even as a Foxe, Polcat, wildcat, or Badgerd will destroye a Warren," wrote George Turberville in *The Noble Art of Venerie* (1575), "so will the Otter destroy all the fishe in your pondes, if he once have found the waye to them."

The animal's extravagant habit of killing more than it needed no doubt contributed to its savage reputation. There was certainly little motivation to hunt the otter for food: in the mid-eighteenth century, the Welsh naturalist Thomas Pennant visited Carthusian monks in Dijon, France. Forbidden from eating meat, in a wily maneuver the famished monks classified the otter as fish, and dined on its flesh daily. Pennant witnessed the food being prepared and described the meat as "excessively rank and fishy." Thomas Fairfax described it as "both cold and filthy . . . and therefore not fit to be eaten," although he later mentions that "there are those in England, who lately have highly valued an otter-pie, much good may do them with it."

In the High Middle Ages under Plantagenet rule, the official title of the King's Otterer was introduced to oversee the extermination of the mammal from the waterways of England. In return for an annual salary and estates in Buckinghamshire (a manor named Otterer's Fee), the royal otterer maintained a pack of "otter dogges" to safeguard the nation's fish stocks; the earliest recorded mention of such an anti-otter squad is from 1157. The position of King's Otterer continued to exist into the Hanoverian period. Henry II appointed his own, Roger Follo, and in 1422 Henry VI appointed William Melbourne as "Valet of our Otter-Hounds," paying him tuppence a day to organize the hunts.

These were carried out on foot—the terrain being too varied for horses—and were physically exhausting. A typical day's chase could last up to seven hours and take the otter hunters across thirty miles of rivers and fields. Because a large part of it involved getting soaked, otter-hunting season was designated April to October, which unfortunately coincided with their breeding phase, meaning many of the otters fleeing the dogs were pregnant (a fact that when revealed would contribute to the turn in public favor much later).

From the beginning, dogs were used to track the scent and seize the animals, in what was thought to be a fair fight. But in the early days of the sport the huntsmen also carried the "otter grain," an unusual barbed trident six to twelve feet long. The multibladed design was an effective solution to the problem of water refraction, giving the spearman three chances of skewering his fleet prey, its nasty barb described by J. W. Carleton in his *Sporting Sketch Book* (1842) as "so constructed that, being driven into the hide of the quarry, it expands and gives out two hooks, which effectually prevent the hold of the spear being destroyed by any efforts of the animal to release itself." In *The Chace* (1735), William Somerville dramatically recounts an otter hunt by spear, the ending of which is particularly vivid:

A detail from the engraving "Hunting ye Otter" in R. Blome's
The Gentleman's Recreation (1686).

Again the crowd attack. That spear has pierc'd
His neck; the crimson waves confess the wound.
Fix'd is the bearded lance, unwelcome guest,
Where-e'er he flies; with him it sinks beneath,
With him it mounts; sure guide to ev'ry foe.
Inly he groans, nor can his tender wound
Bear the cold stream. Lo! to yon sedgy bank
He creeps disconsolate; his num'rous foes
Surround him, hounds and men. Pierc'd thro' and thro',
On pointed spears they lift him high in air;
Wriggling he hangs, and grins, and bites in vain:
Bid the loud horns, in gayly-warbling strains,
Proclaim the felon's fate; he dies, he dies.

Though cherished by some for the strength and skill it demanded, use of the otter grain was later viewed as unsporting by otter hunters and was phased out in the nineteenth century. Despite mounting opposition from animal rights organizations, otter hunts in England were popular right up to 1978, when the mammal was finally listed as a protected species.

Interestingly, the ill feeling toward the otter wasn't a total global antipathy: in ancient Persia the animal was held sacred by the Zoroastrian people, who classified the killing of the creature as a heinous crime. They would even bury with ceremony any dead otter they came across. There were eighteen punishments for the man found guilty of lutracide (murder of "the water-dog"), which included being forced to atone by killing 10,000 corpse-flies, 10,000 frogs, 10,000 snakes, and 10,000 worms. Other reparations included carrying 10,000 loads of wood to the sacred fire, and relinquishing land and property—including any daughters—to "godly men."

ICE TENNIS

Tennis on ice, sometimes referred to as "ten-ice," to groans in the room, was most popular in New York in 1912, when several local tennis clubs together hatched a plan to make their sport as popular in wintertime as it was in summer. To create the ice tennis playing area, they simply flooded their outdoor courts and waited for the water to freeze. After the lines had been painted on and the nets erected with portable posts with weighted bases, the game was ready for its "ten-ice" skaters. This was a niche crowd

The Victorian attire shown in this *Punch* illustration
from 1876 was probably not ideal for ice tennis.

considerably smaller than that of regular tennis, as the sport required of its participants an advanced level of both tennis and skating skill, if they hoped to survive longer than a few minutes. Doubles matches were the preferred form of play, for it was simply too much for one person to cover the area without the aid of friction.

Once accustomed to the demands of sudden braking and awkward lunging, the players began to have fun and sing of its virtues, and it was hoped that clubs across the country would follow suit by also inundating their surfaces. The problem was that it was not a sport accessible or friendly to amateurs, for even the best players would frequently take a tumble. Unlike the grass or clay court surfaces beneath, the ice forgave few errors. "None but the best of skaters could hope to play this game," wrote one journalist. The ball also had a tendency to skid rather than bounce on the ice, a challenge relished by some but which for most was one frustration too many. Demonstration matches crop up in city records from time to time, with a match even played at Madison Square Garden in 1927, but the bruising sport never managed to shake off its novelty status, and time was soon called on the experiment.

THE ICE VELOCIPEDE

In the 1860s, both Europe and America were gripped by a particular vehicular craze: the velocipede. Today we know its surviving form as the bicycle, which possessed other nicknames at the time, such as the "dandy horse" (due to its popularity with the style-obsessed men about town), the "hobby horse," and the "swift walker." The model produced by the French Michaux company, which was made with a wooden frame and metal-rimmed wheels, was known as "the bone-shaker." However, in this early period the two-wheeled pedaled type was only one of several different varieties of velocipede.

Having watched the popularity of the two-wheeled velocipede soar, various inventors experimented with its design, in particular adding and subtracting wheels in the hope of hitting on an exciting alternative that would capture the public's imagination. The monowheel (see page 156) is one example of this "if it ain't broke, let's break it" philosophy, and, though marvelously eccentric, it failed to rival the reliability of the bicycle. An even lesser known child of this frantic period of invention was the ice velocipede.

"The Ice Velocipede is, as might be anticipated, an American

The ice velocipede, taken from Joseph Firth Bottomley's
brilliantly titled book of 1869.

idea," wrote the English barrister Joseph Firth Bottomley in one of the earliest books on bicycling, the tremendously titled *The Velocipede, Its Past, Its Present, & Its Future: How to Ride a Velocipede— "Straddle a Saddle, then Paddle and Skedaddle"* (1869). It consisted of a front-pedaled wheel that dragged behind it two razor-sharp metal skates that balanced the rider upright in considerable discomfort, for it appeared at a time when velocipedes were of a purely metal construction. The wheel was studded to grip the surface of the ice, allowing the rider to build impressive speed on solidified lakes and rivers. While considered to have potential usefulness in the northern parts of the United States and Canada, there was, on the other hand, little appeal for velocipede enthusiasts* in countries of milder climates, much to the remorse of Bottomley, who noted:

> Those who have driven this machine tell us, that the pleasure to be derived from it, is little, if at all inferior, to that which is derived from skating, and if this be so, we can only regret that our humid climate prevents our adding it to the few out-door enjoyments of the winter season.

However, the obvious flaw in the design was apparent even to those watching through their fingers from the shoreline: the thing

---

* There was no official term for the velocipede enthusiast at the time—the sport was nascent, after all—and "cyclist" was not to arrive for some years. Disregarding the more obvious choice of "velocipedist," Bottomley instead proposed a label which we are assured has become quite common across the Atlantic, viz., "Velocipedestrianisticalistinarianologist." As we expect to have some very learned readers, we recommend this word to their study, and if they can make it a "household word," why so much the better.

was simply too heavy, and the rider ran the very real risk of plunging to his death through every patch of thin ice.

ITALIAN CAT HEAD BUTTING

Continuing the theme of feline abuse, in seventeenth-century Italy a popular game at fairs was to string a cat up and charge it down while wearing a spiked helmet. This barbarism, however, was the successor of an even more vicious diversion.

Giovanni Miniati da Prato's *Narrazione e disegno della terra di Prato di Toscana*, published in 1596, is a cultural study of the Tuscan province of Prato. Of particular interest are the descriptions of the games and sports organized as entertainment at annual festivals. The harsh demands of daily medieval life were effective inurements to brutality, and so as one might expect, these celebrations were savage affairs featuring various forms of animal-baiting, the bloodier the better. In the village square, for example, a pig was contained in a large pen. Men armed with clubs entered the arena and chased the animal, eventually trapping it in a corner and beating it to death "among the loud laughter of those present."

Even more extreme, though, was the cat head butting. A live cat, specially selected for the event, was brought out and nailed to a post or tree. Then young male contestants with freshly shaven heads lined up and had their hands bound behind their backs. They knelt in front of the cat and, "to the sound of trumpets," took turns in battering the life out of the animal with their foreheads. The trick was to avoid the creature's claws, which were free to slash cheeks and gouge eyeballs. When it was over, the men were celebrated by the crowd as they stood covered in a mixture of their own blood and that of the lifeless animal.

KOTTABOS

Modern society owes much to the innovation of the ancient Greeks in the fields of philosophy, politics, medicine, art, and almost every other significant aspect of developed civilization. But what of their off-duty activities, when the sun had set on a productive day's musing and the mind began to turn to more frivolous and booze-fueled entertainment?

Kottabos, sometimes cottabus, was a drinking competition of skill and decadence, popular in the fourth and fifth centuries BC, in which contestants flung the contents of their wine cups at targets in basins with remarkable accuracy. Maintaining a reclining position at the dining table, the player would deftly flick his chalice with his right hand, sending the remaining wine and lees flying through the air in one unbroken liquid missile. This, and the noise made upon impact, was known as $\lambda \acute{\alpha} \tau \alpha \xi$ (latax). The best players had the aim of a spitting cobra and were held in a similar level of regard as those who threw the javelin. The game was heavily gambled upon, and because of the element of luck involved, the performance of each kottabos contestant was viewed as an omen of their future successes, especially in affairs of the heart.

There were two main modes of play. In the first, $K\acute{o}\tau\tau\alpha\beta o\varsigma$ $\delta\iota$ ' $\acute{o}\xi\upsilon\beta\acute{\alpha}\varphi\omega\nu$ (kottabos with oxybaphon), the targets of the wine flingers were small saucers that bobbed in a basin filled with water.

A young man is shown playing kottabos on a kylix (drinking cup) from 480–460 BC, discovered in Chiusi, Italy. (*Marie-Lan Nguyen*)

Whoever managed to sink the highest number of these plates with his vinous lobbings was the winner of the κοττάβιον (cottabium, or prize), which was usually a confection. The second variation, Κότταβος κατακτός (sunken kottabos), centered on a more complex target of two differently sized saucers placed on a pole at separate heights, with a bronze figurine beneath. The goal was to fill the small saucer at the top and cause the whole thing to collapse onto the figure.

Kottabos was widespread throughout ancient Greece, but by the Roman and Alexandrian periods the scant references to it suggest the game had fallen out of fashion, perhaps in part due to the sartorial challenges presented to its participants in an era before dry cleaning.

LAST COUPLE IN HELL

Also known as barley-break, this was a rural British game played among the barley stacks of farmyards from the sixteenth to the eighteenth centuries. It required the participation of mixed couples, and as such was the favorite of young men looking for an excuse to roll around in the hay with the object of their affections. The playing field was divided into three parts, with the central area nicknamed hell. After drawing lots to determine roles, a couple stood in each section and held hands; it was the job of the pair in hell to catch the others as they attempted to cross from one end to the other. Whoever was caught would then replace them in hell. The name barley-break came from the tendency of the couples to evade their captors by letting go or "breaking" from each other's grasp, something the couple in hell were forbidden to do.

The earliest mention of the game is made by Henry Machyn in his diary entry of April 19, 1557, in which he records playing a game of "barlye breyke." In Scotland, the game was called "barla-bracks," and, according to John Jamieson's 1808 Scottish dictionary, was "generally played by young people in a cornyard, hence its name, barla-bracks, about the stacks."

Particularly notable about the game is how often it served as a handy metaphor for writers and poets of the era. The seventeenth-century poet Robert Herrick (1591–1674), for example, devotes a poem to the game entitled "Barley-break; or, Last in Hell":

We two are last in hell; what may we fear,
To be tormented, or kept pris'ners here?

Alas, if kissing be of plagues the worst,
We'll wish in hell we had been last and first.

Elsewhere, in Thomas Middleton and William Rowley's 1622 Jacobean tragedy *The Changeling*, the term is used with sexual connotation, as an adulterer tells his cuckold, "I coupled with your mate at barley-break; now we are left in hell"; while in James Shirley's 1633 comedy *The Bird in a Cage*, a suitor asks his companion: "Shall's to barlibreak?" to which she replies: "I was in hell last; 'tis little less to be in a petticoat sometimes." The game fell from favor as Britain moved into the more reserved Victorian era, when such a hands-on approach to courting was viewed with disapproval (and today we have nightclubs, so perhaps a revival isn't likely anytime soon).

LION-BAITING

One of the earliest mentions of dogs being played off against a lion for entertainment comes from the Roman historian Claudius Aelianus (ca. AD 175–235). He describes how Alexander the Great was gifted 150 fearsome hunting dogs by the Indian King Sopeithes, ruler of an area around Jech Doab in Punjab. The monarch organized for the two weakest dogs to be pitted against a lion, to show the strength of the breed. The menagerie attendants first released a stag for the animals to play with, but the dogs ignored it; then a wild boar, but again it held no interest for the canines, who even turned their noses up at a bear. However, when the lion was released into the ring the dogs recognized a worthy adversary and set upon it. One of the dogs managed to clamp its mouth around the throat of the great beast and began to choke the life out of it. Sopeithes ordered that the lion be released, but the immense strength of the dogs (purported to be offspring of tigers) was matched by their determination to kill. A servant hacked at the dog's tail with a scimitar, but still it held on. The man then severed its leg (at which point Alexander protested, but was placated with the offer of three more dogs), yet still the dog held on, until with a final slice the servant decapitated the dog, its body falling away to leave the head still attached to the cat, jaws locked around the throat, tenacious to the end.

Because of the rare exoticism of the participant, the sport was usually reserved as a special entertainment for the royal court: James I, for example, organized a match between a lion and three of the bravest mastiffs in the land, which were duly collected by Edward Alleyn, master of the Bear Garden. As was usual in lion-baiting, the fight took place inside the lion's cage, with the dogs released one by one. In this instance, however, the lion was keen to be the initiator of the proceedings and snatched up the first dog through the bars, killing it quickly. The second leapt into the fray but met the same end, and the third, though managing to latch onto the cat by its lower jaw, also failed to triumph. The lion retreated to lick its wounds, and the third dog escaped, later to be cared for by the king's son, Henry, who reportedly said of his new pet, "He had fought the king of the wild animals and should never again have to fight baser creatures." The dog spent the rest of his life as a pampered canine of the court.

Through the centuries, further lion-baitings were occasionally recorded, with Vienna enjoying the unofficial status (and dubi-

Theodore Lane's "The Fight between the Lion Wallace & the dogs
Tinker & Ball in the Factory Yard in the Town of Warwick."

ous honor) of being the lion-baiting capital of the world in the 1790s. But it was the lion fights organized in Britain in 1825 by a traveling showman named George Wombwell that were to be the sport's grand finale. On the outskirts of Warwick, in the Old Factory Yard, Wombwell and his mobile menagerie staged a battle between his prize lion, Nero, and a pack of Staffordshire bull terriers, led by the ferocious Sammy. In front of a capacity crowd, who had paid as much as three guineas each for admittance, for twenty minutes Nero grappled with the stubborn Staffies, until finally Sammy employed the tactic of his forebears and clamped onto the lion's jaw, refusing to let go. The two were eventually separated, and Sammy was declared the winner. The dog was later presented with a medal.

In the same week, a second match was staged between a set of bulldogs and the formidable Wallace, the first African lion bred in Britain. In this case the dogs were greatly outmatched, and as the lion tossed his stock around like rag dolls, the owner of the bulldogs was said to have cried out at Wombwell: "There, you see how you've gammoned me to have the best dog in England killed!"

After news spread of the lion and dog matches, there was a national outcry at the treatment of the noble creatures, and the sport was quickly suppressed. Wallace went on to live a relatively peaceful life in captivity, the only blip on his otherwise spotless record occurring in 1827 when he ripped the arm off a member of the public who had tried to pet him through the bars at a fair. Upon his death, Wallace's body was transported by stagecoach to Saffron Walden Museum in Essex, where he was stuffed and remains on display to this day.

MAN-BAITING

It was a practice that took place in the deepest shadows of the underworld, in smoke-filled basements and airless cellars of nondescript buildings on forgettable streets. The gamblers who came were in search of the thrill of a bloody spectacle more exotic than even the lion fight or the monkey-bait. In these hidden arenas they found a visceral, primal fight where men fought pit bull terriers with their bare hands. Here dog bit man, and man bit back.

For obvious reasons, historical records of these events are few and far between, but they do exist. For example, *The Sporting Magazine* of September 1801 features an illustration of such a scene entitled "The Gentleman and the Bulldog," describing it as "an engagement that took place (for a wager) some time ago," and providing a brief summary of the match:

On the sett too, the Bull Dog so far mastered his adversary as to bring him to the ground; and, notwithstanding the animal's mouth was nearly closed by the muzzle, he fastened on the body of the gentleman; and, if not instantly taken off, would have torn out his bowels.

Most vivid, though, is the story of a dwarf named Brummy pitted against a bulldog called Physic in a back-alley fighting den in Hanley, Staffordshire. The tale was recorded by the journalist James Greenwood in his 1875 social exploration *Low-Life Deeps—An Account of the Strange Fish to Be Found There.*

Greenwood was led down into a basement filled with a crowd ranging from off-duty quarry workers to noble gentlemen in cutaway coats and snuff-colored trousers. "But the person whose personage chiefly attracted my attention," wrote Greenwood, "was a

"The Gentleman and the Bulldog," as shown in
The Sporting Magazine, 1801.

dwarf—a man of at least middle age, judging from his grizzled grey hair, and the enormous size of his head and ears, but certainly not more than four feet and a half in height, yet with tremendous hands and feet and bandy legs." This was Brummy, who stripped to the waist, showing off an impressive collection of muscle and scars, and proceeded to rub himself down with oil.

Then entered Physic, a "hideous-jowled dirty white bulldog," who tried to lunge at Brummy as soon as he saw him. Both competitors were chained to stakes, Physic by the collar, Brummy by a waist strap. "I dislike rum," recalled Greenwood at this point, "yet . . . I was positively grateful when the young sociable pitman by my side pressed a 'nip' on my acceptance." The rules of the fight were established: victory went to whoever bit or knocked the other "out of time," i.e., into a state in which they were unable to resume the fight within sixty seconds. Physic was the favorite, and by now was "frenzied with passion to that degree that tears trickled down his blunt nose."

The opponents faced off, both on all fours. The organizer cried, "Let go!" and the dog flew at the dwarf, who remained just outside the length of the animal's chain, and as it fought against its tether, punched it in the head. The dog was stunned but recovered, and this continued for round after round. By the tenth, the bulldog's head was badly swollen and Brummy was bleeding profusely from gashes in his forearms and torso. Finally, in the eleventh round the dog lunged and Brummy dealt it a tremendous uppercut, sending it flying into a wall, and "the wretch who had so disgraced what aspect of humanity was in him was declared the victor."

MAN VS. WOMAN COMBAT

Hans Talhoffer was a fifteenth-century German fencing expert, fighting master, and mercenary. Little biographical detail survives of the great swordsman: he was born ca. 1410 and died sometime after 1482, and his name crops up occasionally in various city records, indicating a peripatetic career of tutelage and contest adjudication. Despite this, his reputation survives thanks to the extraordinary illustrated manuals he produced, which feature instruction on a hugely diverse range of martial arts and weaponry. One such manual is his *Fechtbuch* (Fight Book, or Fencing Book) created in 1459 and referred to as MS Thott.290.2°. The original copy is preserved in Det Kongelige Bibliotek in Copenhagen, Denmark, where only a handful of visitors have been allowed access to it. The book is a comprehensive guide to sword-fighting techniques, but in its three hundred pages it goes on to cover bizarre areas of battle, with wonderfully vivid illustrations of siege weaponry and even early Renaissance-era diving apparatus.

In particular, a series of nine illustrations is especially eye-catching, because they show a man and a woman clashing in a bloody fight inside a purpose-built ring. The event is a judicial trial by combat, a Germanic legal custom invoked when no other legal recourse was available to resolve a dispute.*

In Talhoffer's instructional guide, the issue of the male physi-

---

* One of the earliest known judicial duels was fought in 1127 between Guy, a knight who was accused of participating in the assassination of Charles the Benevolent of Flanders, and his accuser, a knight named Herrmann. After fighting for two hours with various weapons, the men began wrestling each other, until Herrmann brought the matter to a close by ripping away Guy's genitals.

cal advantage is countered with a hole cut into the floor of the ring in which the man stands, the ring rising up to his waist. The male combatant is armed with a sword, the woman with what appears to be a rock wrapped in a sheet, forming a kind of cudgel, and both are dressed in the same one-piece costume that covers their heads. The series of images depicts the man, in his reduced position, being battered, bent over backwards and choked, face-gouged, and put in a headlock. He manages to get in a few good shots of his own, slashing the woman's calves and at one point dragging her down headfirst into the hole with him. The caption of the final image, in which both contestants lie bleeding on the floor, translates as "Here they make an end of each other."

MOB FOOTBALL

European football once existed in a form so violent and destructive that royal decrees were issued forbidding any involvement, and its players faced threats of excommunication from the Church. In its early medieval form, commonly referred to as "mob football," the game has more in common with pitched battle than it does with the sport today known as the "beautiful game." It was usually played on religious holidays—Shrove Tuesday being a particularly popular time—for this was when large gatherings occurred. After the church service, the people would make their way out into the fields surrounding their town or village, with someone bringing an inflated pig's bladder for the purpose. The number of players was unlimited—whole villages competed against each other. The pitch was unmarked, save for the goals. These were usually established with posts in the home village of each team; quite often the balcony or yard of the local church was used, to the fury of clergymen.

The ball was hurled into the air and the match began. There were few rules and no limits on aggression, just the understanding that any tactic was permitted to force the bladder into the enemy's goal. As a result, the violence was frequent and bloody, with even deaths known to happen. When a match was due to be staged, shopkeepers closed for the day, in part because there was likely to be little business, but mainly to prevent their stores being destroyed in the inevitable brawling that was to come. The aggression is evinced by some of the earliest references to the game. Dating to around the twelfth century, in *Das Chronicon Montis Sereni*, a note is made of a boy being kicked so hard during a German game of football that he died. A fourteenth-century Nottinghamshire friar described the mass scrummage:

> In this game young people propel a large ball forward, but not by throwing it, but by kicking the ball and rolling it on the ground with their feet. It is a rather horrible game, I must say, vulgar, unworthy, and less worthwhile than any other game, which seldom ends without some kind of mishap . . .

In 1314, one of the earliest mentions of the sport's name is made by Nicholas de Farndone, Lord Mayor of the City of London, who issued a ban:

> Forasmuch as there is great noise in the city caused by hustling over large foot balls in the fields of the public from which many

evils might arise which God forbid: we command and forbid on behalf of the king, on pain of imprisonment, such game to be used in the city in the future.

Over in France, a similar sport known as *la soule* was just as popular, and just as dangerous. As well as distracting the public from practicing skills such as archery, which were vital in training the populace in times of frequent war, the Church abhorred the game's usurpation of the Sabbath. Just as in England, the clergy lambasted the practice; in a resolution from 1440, the bishop of Tréguier threatened ballplayers with excommunication, declaring:

It has been decided that these dangerous and harmful games should be forbidden on account of the bad feeling, ill will and animosity which this amusement, apparently designed for recreation, arouses in men's hearts, and which provides a pernicious occasion for fermenting hatred. We have been informed by several ecclesiastics that in the territory of the parishes administered by them, a dangerous game has been played on holidays and weekdays with a large ball, which is usually called mellat. This has already caused many scandals, and it is obvious that it will cause more if we do not rectify the matter.

In Italy, a more refined form of the ballgame was popular, known as *giucco del calcio*, or *calcio fiorentino*. This was usually played in winter, in the Piazza di Santa Croce, the Piazza di Santo Spirito, or the Piazza di Santa Maria Novella (one match was even held on the frozen River Arno in 1490), on a pitch marked out with fencing. The game began with the umpire hurling the ball against the wall of one of the nearby houses. As it bounced back into the pitch, the two twenty-seven-man teams attempted to drive it into the goal using both feet and fists, with a healthy amount of shoving, kicking, and punching encouraged. In contrast to early English football, here the game was the preserve of the aristocratic. It was a Venetian, Antonio Scaino, who, in 1555, produced the first book dedicated to ball games. In *Trattato del giucco della palla*, he describes the game with a reverence undiminished in soccer fans ever since, praising the act of *caccia* (scoring goals) as a *glorioso fatto*, or "glorious deed."

An illustration of a game of *calcio*, as played in sixteenth-century Italy, taken from Henry René d'Allemagne's *Sports et Jeux d'adresse* (1903).

MONKEY-FIGHTING

Rats, ducks, bears, lions, and even men—no one could accuse the animal-baiters of the seventeenth and eighteenth centuries of a lack of inventiveness when it came to organizing adversaries for their fighting dogs. Any exotic creature offering a novel spectacle was seized upon, for the lucrative gambling opportunities drew to the pits crowds of every background, from dockers to dukes.

Wildly popular but of considerable rarity were instances of monkey-baiting, in which primates imported from all over the globe (usually "Old World" primates of Asia and Africa) were pitted against champion fighting terriers and other animals in battles to the death. Each species brought with it a different fighting style, and monkeys in particular made for an intelligent and tactical foe.

A notable example of this was the twelve-rat match that took place in Manchester in 1880 between Mr. Benson's revered fox terrier Turk and Mr. Lewis's monkey. The dog was well known to the crowd; with his proven track record in quick rat killing, he was heavily favored by the odds. Turk went first, and indeed turned in a splendid performance, killing the requisite amount of vermin in an impressive time. Now for the monkey. Another twelve rats were brought forward and dumped into the ring. Mr. Lewis then placed his monkey down among them, withdrew a large hammer from his coat, and handed it to his fighter. The monkey proceeded to pound the life out of the animals to win the match in record time. For months afterwards, there was debate as to whether a rule should be introduced to explicitly forbid monkeys wielding weapons.

Although the average fighting monkey possessed half the weight of the average fighting dog, the canine's victory was never certain, for the tough skin and powerful paws of the simian could sometimes swing the battle. Animals victorious in the baiting pits quickly became celebrities. The more fights they won, the more money they made for their fans, and the wider their fame spread. These stars were usually the terriers, like Mr. Swift's Billie, Mr. Dixon's Toe Biter, and Tom Cribb's monstrous pit bull bitch, Puss. But every now and again one of the baited got the upper hand and gained instant notoriety. In the world of monkey-baiting, the most famous of these underdog champions was the mighty Jacco Macacco.

Jacco's provenance and species were matters of debate. Some said he was a gibbon from the African continent; others claimed he was of Italian origin. Whatever the color of his passport, his fur was black, his teeth were sharp, and he quickly developed a lethally effective fighting technique that saw him cut a swath through the terrier population of London. In his *Pictures of Sporting Life and Character* (1860), Lord William Pitt Lennox charts Jacco Macacco's path to celebrity. After getting his start in the dog rings of Portsmouth, Jacco was brought to London to fight in the pits at Chick Lane and Tottenham Court Road, where he "took the conceit out of some of the very stoutest breed of dogs that this country could boast of." Jacco also began to attack his owner, who, perhaps sensing he was soon to go the way of the pit bulls, decided to sell him to Charles Aistrop, the owner of the Westminster pit, and it was here that Jacco became a star. Punters came from far and wide to see the famous dog destroyer, whose preferred method of dispatch was to climb onto the back of his opponent and tear out its windpipe with his teeth. The animal fell down dead, and Jacco stood proud in victory, covered in blood, a fearsome sight. In this way he was able to work through more than ten dogs a night; for in the ring with Jacco Macacco, an opponent lasted on average about ninety seconds.

Like all good legends, the conclusion of Jacco's story is shrouded in as much mystery as its beginning. His last fight, which Aistrop claimed took place on June 13, 1821, was against the celebrated Puss, who had a considerable weight advantage over the monkey. The result of the match is disputed. An MP named Richard Martin claimed that Jacco triumphed over Puss but in the process had his lower jaw torn off and died shortly after; however, Martin made this assertion in parliamentary session, using the story as context for an animal cruelty bill he was attempting to introduce. Aistrop confirmed that Jacco had indeed triumphed over Puss,

"Fight with the Ape," by Thomas Landseer, shows Jacco Macacco taking on Puss in what was to be the famous monkey's final contest.

155

but insisted that neither creature had died. Puss went into retirement, and Jacco, he said, passed away fifteen months after the fight from an unrelated illness, later to be stuffed and sold.

THE MONOWHEEL

The monowheel, or monocycle, is, as the name suggests, a vehicle consisting of a single giant wheel. A dream shared by inventors and engineers for centuries, it has an extensive developmental history. The unveiling of each attempt at perfecting the design was always accompanied by headlines hailing it as the "transport of tomorrow," poised to take the world by storm. And yet despite its appealing form, the vehicle never quite found mainstream popularity thanks to one persistent flaw—the design.

Take, for instance, the most striking incarnation of the monowheel: the Dynasphere. This was the creation of physicist and electrification expert John Archibald Purves, a Fellow of the Royal Society of Edinburgh and devoted inventor, who revealed the vehicle to the British public in 1932. The design of the Dynasphere was relatively simple: the driver's seat, controls, and engine sat on rails, themselves inside a ten-foot, thousand-pound circular cage of iron latticework. As this outer wheel revolved, the inner unit would (theoretically) remain level. Perhaps the most curious aspect of the monstrous beast was the relatively minor amount of power needed to reach its top speed of 30 mph: a two-cylinder air-cooled Douglas engine of 6 hp was controlled with a three-speed gearbox. There was even the option of reverse. Steering, though, was slightly trickier, requiring the driver to lean into the direction he wished to turn. The controls did allow him to shift the inner unit to the outside of the outer wheel to some degree, thereby tilting the machine, but it was common to see the driver also craning his torso out the unprotected sides of his cockpit as part of basic maneuvering. Deceleration was achieved simply by switching off the engine and gradually rolling to a halt.

When the machine debuted at the Brooklands racetrack in Surrey, it was with a grand introduction by Mrs. Purves, who told reporters: "Gravity itself is our motive power, and pulls us along. We can start on ice, we can start on mud or slime, because we are not trusting to push the wheel round to get ourselves going." As the Dynasphere rolled out toward the track, the onlookers followed closely behind. With the engine roaring, the giant wheel raced backed and forth along the track with its driver rocking

Testing the Dynasphere at Brean Sands,
Weston-super-Mare, in Somerset in 1932. (*Getty Images*)

unsteadily inside. It was a sensation. When he tested it on the flat sands of Brean in Weston-super-Mare, Purves drove the alien machine along the rural roads of Weston. The sight certainly made an impression on the locals, although one schoolboy was left underwhelmed by the machine's performance: "One day in the 1930s," the witness later said, "I went to the beach and saw a man trying to drive a huge wheel across the sands. It wasn't very successful and wobbled about. I have always wondered what it was or whether I imagined it." It is of this event that we have a stunning and iconic photographic record.

Purves was said to have been inspired by original sketches by Leonardo da Vinci, and perhaps this was indeed the case, but there were in fact more recent monowheel designs of which he surely would have been aware. Most enthusiasts trace the design back to 1869, when the first patents for such a device were registered; but, if explored further, an obscure 1518 woodcut by Hans Burgkmair becomes rather significant. It forms part of the *Triumphzug*, or *The Triumphal Procession*, a series of woodcut prints 177 feet long produced by Burgkmair, Albrecht Dürer, and others. The work was commissioned by Emperor Maximilian I in the early sixteenth century to celebrate his own magnificence, and the images record a tremendous procession held in his honor, featuring a parade of courtiers, troops, animals, and vehicles packed like clown cars. Together with its sister sections, *Triumphal Arch* and *Large Triumphal Carriage*, it was designed as a giant frieze that would—according to Maximilian's own documents—"grace the walls of council chambers and great halls of the empire, proclaiming for posterity the noble aims of their erstwhile ruler."

The truth is, however, that no such procession ever took

place. Maximilian couldn't afford one. But what he lacked in funds he made up for in propagandistic shrewdness, and allegedly responded to any questioning of his spending with the philosophy "He who does not provide for his memory while he lives will not be remembered after his death, so that this person will be forgotten when the bell tolls. And hence the money I spend for my memory will not be lost."

Amid the great work, wedged between partying bands of jousters, jesters, soldiers, elephants, and even griffins, can be found the panel in question. It appears to show an early form of tread-wheel carriage, powered by courtiers running along the track. The escort to the left engages the wheel with a staff, possibly to brake or steady the counterweighted rostrum holding the precious royal cargo. As the men scrabble like hamsters, the emperor sits on his throne, surrounded by his family.

Developing this "human hamster wheel" theme, the next notable event in monowheel history is provided by British politician and inventor Richard Lovell Edgeworth (1744–1817), who wrote in his memoirs of a machine he built in 1769:

A huge hollow wheel made very light, withinside of which, in a barrel of six feet diameter, a man should walk. Whilst he stepped thirty inches, the circumference of the large wheel, or rather wheels, would revolve five feet on the ground; and as the machine was to roll on planks, and on a plane somewhat inclined, when once the vis inertia of the machine should be overcome, it would carry on the man within it as fast as he could possibly walk . . . It was not finished; I had not yet finished it with the means of stopping or moderating its motion.

The reason Edgeworth never finished his vehicle was because one night a "young lad" gained entrance to its unguarded storage space, hopped inside it, and took off down a hill. Unbeknown to the joyrider, however, the slope led to a deep quarry. When the boy realized what lay ahead he leapt from the contraption, and the machine flew over the cliff to be dashed to pieces on the pit floor. Edgeworth was devastated:

> The next day, when I came to look for my machine, intending to try it upon some planks, which had been laid for it, I found, to my no small disappointment, that the object of all my labors and my hopes was lying at the bottom of a chalk-pit, broken into a thousand pieces. I could not at that time afford to construct another wheel of that sort, and I cannot therefore determine what might have been the success of my scheme.

Later, in 1869, there was a flurry of monowheel activity when several patents were filed by different inventors around the United States—some even on the same day—for designs of vehicles that could now be more aptly termed monocycles. (This sudden popularity can be attributed to an article on velocipedes that appeared in *Scientific American* in March 1869.) One such patent was that of Richard C. Hemming of New Haven, Connecticut, who submitted a futuristic design that was nicknamed the "Flying Yankee Velocipede." What is most notable about Hemming's design is the fact that it is propelled by hand. If we examine the following illustration of Hemming's machine, taken from J. T. Goddard's *The Velocipede: Its History, Varieties, and*

Illustration of Hemming's "Flying Yankee Velocipede,"
taken from J. T. Goddard's book.

Practice (1869), we can see that the driver's feet appear to rest on a kind of rigid treadle, and therefore were indeed unlikely to contribute to propulsion.

Hemming claimed that one rotation of the handwheel was equal to one rotation of the main wheel, but according to the measurements this is more likely to have required three complete turns of the hand crank, meaning that for the operator to achieve the boasted speed of 25 mph he would have had to spin the handwheel at a furious and improbable rate of forty revolutions per minute (before collapsing in a panting heap).

Summing up the 1869 monowheel craze, Joseph Firth Bottomley, author of *The Velocipede, Its Past, Its Present, & Its Future*, wrote:

We are not aware that any of these machines have been hitherto seen at large, nor what method has been hit upon for guiding them . . . [and] what would become of the unfortunate inmate in case he "collided" with a cart, or any similar obstacle does not sufficiently appear.

Discussing a design that placed the rider atop the wheel, the same author gives an insight into how the excitement at the possibilities of the vehicle turned rational men into "monocyclomaniacs" with a "bigger, faster!" approach to engineering that served the *Titanic* so well:

For our part, we do not see why this inventor need be so mod-est. Why restrict the diameter to twelve feet, or the speed to twenty-five miles per hour? If the principle be good, why not extend its application, and let the rider have a thirty-foot wheel, and a speed of sixty miles an hour? The difference in safety can-not be great.

Over the years, inventors continued to refine the monowheel design, and hundreds of different models were revealed. So why did the monocycle never take off as a popular method of trans-port? Is this a grave injustice in need of immediate rectification, as it is tempting to conclude? No, not really. As exciting as a ride on the vehicle must have been, it was accompanied by all sorts of drawbacks. For the Dynasphere, the most significant (and frankly, hilarious) of these was the high risk of "gerbiling." This was the name given to the phenomenon occurring when the vehicle was too sharply accelerated or braked, causing the inner carriage to rotate 360 degrees, spinning the driver around like a load of laundry on a heavy rinse cycle, no doubt reacquainting him with his breakfast as he attempted to regain control.

Despite continual refinements to the design, monocyclists kept encountering the same problems. The basic instability of a man perched on or inside a giant wheel was never quite solved, and it took only a few instances of high-speed tipping to put off prospective riders. The visibility issue, too, was a head-scratcher— shifting in your seat to see around the giant rim in front of you led back to the tipping problem. Another unfavorable aspect of the vehicle was the lack of room for passengers. Purves attempted to address this matter with a follow-up design to his Dynasphere. Despite the underwhelming response to his first invention, the good doctor introduced a scale model of his next planned project: a larger, glass-carriaged Dynasphere capable of transporting up to five people. Thankfully, for both pedestrians and the Purves family members who doubtless would have been roped into testing the thing, funding for the development of the rolling lawsuit was never secured.

NAUMACHIAE

*N*aumachiae were giant sea battles reenacted in flooded Roman arenas. Condemned criminals and captured prisoners of war fought to the death as they played out famous naval campaigns for the entertainment of a crowd. The events required sophisticated planning and execution, and as such were performed only with the approval of the emperor to mark special occasions.

In 46 BC, on the orders of Julius Caesar, an enormous basin was dug in the Campus Martius (Field of Mars) outside the walls of Rome and filled with water. For this event (to celebrate the emperor's recent Gallic, Alexandrian, Pontic, and African triumphs), two fleets of biremes, triremes, and quadremes, representing Tyre and Egypt, clashed in a battle of epic scale involving more than six thousand prisoners who played the parts of soldiers and rowers. Also on record is the *naumachia* organized in 40 BC by Sextus Pompey for the entertainment of his troops, which featured prisoners of war fighting to the death to celebrate his victory over Salvidienus Rufus and the occupation of Sicily.

Naumachiae are thought to date back to the third century BC, when the Roman general Scipio Africanus staged the reenactments using his own troops, as mentioned by Suetonius in his *Life of the Caesars*, and by Cassius Dio in his *Roman History*. Together with his favored general, Marcus Agrippa, Emperor Augustus developed large areas of the Campus Martius for the sport, which included the Baths of Agrippa and also the Stagnum Agrippae (Lake of Agrippa), an ornamental body of water considerably larger than that dug by Julius Caesar, possessing dimensions of 1,800 by 1,200 (Roman) feet and located beside the River Tiber, with water piped in via a newly completed aqueduct.

One of the grandest *naumachiae* ever mounted, though, was that of Claudius in AD 52. To mark the opening of a canal that was to later dry the Fucine Lake, a naval battle between Rhodes and Sicily was staged, consisting of nineteen thousand soldiers manning one hundred ships. Little is known about the specifics of how the sea battles were conducted. Aquatic displays as a whole were popular at the time, and included exhibitions of captured marine curiosities, water ballets, and pantomimes, and so it is possible that the events were entirely theatrical. It is thought that two opposing fleets would face off, but as it is unclear how much of the action was pre-orchestrated, the events are categorized somewhere between sport and theatrical re-creation. How fierce the battles were is also a mystery, although the fact that participants were usually facing imminent execution either way must have meant there was little motivation to participate enthusiastically. Indeed, Tacitus writes about Claudius being forced to dispatch the imperial guard on rafts during a *naumachia* in AD 52 to impel the two sides into fighting.

In terms of venue, as well as the aforementioned basins, natural settings such as lakes and the Rhegium coast were used; but there is also evidence to suggest that the battles were hosted in amphitheaters. For years archaeologists have debated whether the dual-level labyrinth of chambers beneath the Colosseum arena known as the *hypogea* support or disprove the notion that aquatic displays were staged in the arena. Ancient sources indicate that *naumachiae* did indeed take place, but it is thought that for this to have been successful the ships involved must have been smaller in scale. This is especially likely when one takes into consideration the fact that the length of one trireme was nearly half the length of the entire amphitheater. The Colosseum, or the Flavian Amphitheater as it is also known, is thought to have housed these spectacles on its launch. The construction was initiated by Vespasian around AD 73 on the site of an artificial lake built by Nero, and, for its two inauguration ceremonies, aquatic displays were performed each time, according to Martial, who writes in his *Liber spectaculorum* about witnessing fleets, land animals in a naval environment, and carts running upon the water. Despite living much later than the events he describes, and therefore being a slightly less reliable source, Cassius Dio (ca. AD 164–235) wrote about the inauguration of Titus and describes a *naumachia* in the amphitheater:

> For [Titus] suddenly filled this same theater with water and brought in horses and bulls and some other domesticated animals that have been taught to behave in the liquid element just as on land. He also brought in people on ships, who engaged in a sea-fight there, impersonating the Corcyreans and Corinthians; and others gave a similar exhibition outside the city in the grove of Gaius and Lucius, a place Augustus had once excavated for this very purpose.

Dio records another *naumachia* taking place two days later:

> . . . and on the third day a naval battle between three thousand men, followed by an infantry battle. The "Athenians" conquered the "Syracusans" (these were the names the combatants used), made a landing on the islet ["Ortygia"] and assaulted and captured a wall that had been constructed around the monument.

The existing walls of the *hypogea* were first thought to disprove the idea, as they would obstruct such a thing from happening, but it has since been shown that the walls were added much

An engraving of what a *naumachia* might have looked like,
published by Johann Georg Heck, 1844.

later, possibly as late as the Middle Ages, and therefore the early form of the amphitheater would have been capable of holding the events. This is further supported by the discovery that the drains were built as part of the original foundation. However, excavations have still failed to turn up specific evidence of the *naumachiae* being staged in the Colosseum, such as remnants of ships or weapons used.

The *naumachiae* were clearly used more as demonstrations of imperial might than anything else, designed to inspire awe with the sheer scale of the spectacle. Literary evidence suggests that *naumachiae* took place only in Rome and declined in popularity after the first century AD, the last one being recorded in AD 89, though other forms of aquatic displays continued to be in high demand. In particular, an alternative use, the Stagnum Agrippae, was found by Nero, as Tacitus records in his *Annals*:

To give the impression that he enjoyed himself in Rome more than anywhere else, Nero held banquets in public places and used the entire city as if it were his home . . . One time he had a special party boat constructed which was towed around the Pool of Agrippa by other boats, all of them finished in gold and ivory and having for rowers male prostitutes grouped according to their age and erotic specialty. He supplied it with birds and animals imported from distant lands, and sea creatures from as far away as the Atlantic. Brothels were constructed on the shores of the pond and stocked with well-born ladies; on the opposite shore, out in the open, naked prostitutes danced and gestured obscenely.

NEW YORK BULLFIGHTING

It was promised to be the most remarkable spectacle the city of New York had ever seen, and this was a prestige certainly achieved, but not for the reasons the promoters had imagined. It was the summer of 1880, and posters advertising New York's first ever "Grand Bull-Fight" were pasted up all around the city:

At the Central Park Arena, corner One Hundred and Sixteenth-street and Sixth-avenue. The celebrated Toreros, Spanish bull-fighters will give a wonderful performance on Saturday, July 31. Don't fail to go and see it, as you will never have an opportunity to see the wonderful skill of these professional men, who will surprise the public of New-York in their risky feats with the ferocious bulls. At the head of this company the renowned Valdemoro will be present. Six wild Texas bulls will perform. In case of one not being wild enough, it will be replaced by another. No cruelty will be used toward the animals.

The "Central Park Arena" (now the site of a delicatessen) was an empty allotment "up among the shanties," as one reporter put it, in which the promoter Angel Fernandez had constructed a makeshift stadium featuring a circular arena fenced by wooden boards six feet high, seating, and even private boxes. The bulls that were promised to be "ferocious beasts" were collected from a local stockyard, having been "packed in cars for some days, and were pretty well worn out," according to one reporter. Price of entry was steep: $1.50 for adults, 75 cents for children under the age of eight. Nevertheless, the idea enchanted the public, and on the morning of the fight the elevated trains on the West Side Road were packed, and the queues for the two ticket offices extended for entire blocks.

Henry Bergh, the founder of the American Society for the Prevention of Cruelty to Animals, was also in attendance. Upon first learning of the event he had immediately denounced it, but Fernandez had assured him that no harm would come to the animals. The bulls of this *tauromaquia* were not to suffer the stabbing of lances or darts; instead the *toreros* would merely attempt to slap gummed ribbon rosettes to the foreheads of the beasts. Bergh decided to attend and ensure the promise was kept, expressing his reservation to a *New York Herald* reporter that "there seems to be an appetite among men for anything that savors of cruelty . . .

169

If this sport should become popular here, we should soon be reduced to the level of Spanish character and nothing should satisfy the public but blood."

As it transpired, Bergh's fears of a bloodbath and a new national craze were ill-founded. Angel Fernandez was a skilled salesman, but it became apparent that his ability as an event organizer left something to be desired. The bullfighters who entered the ring in full matador costume ("All the colors of the rainbow were represented . . . and one or two colors that the rainbow dreams not of," wrote one journalist) did not quite resemble the heroic imagery associated with their profession. "They were as bad a looking set of men as ever picked a pocket, and looked as if, while they would fight a steer for a dollar and a half, they would cut a throat for a quarter . . ." sniped the *Times* reporter, adding, "No one of them had been shaved, apparently, since the death of the late Pope."*

The fighters bowed to the crowd and took up their positions, awaiting their combatants. The first bull was released into the arena, and the men flourished their capes majestically. The animal made a beeline for the *torero* with the red cape, who immediately turned and leapt over the nearest wall. It was clear that Fernandez's "professional men" knew nothing about bullfighting. The second bull was released, and despite having protective padding on the tips of its horns to prevent any possibility of goring, also succeeded in terrifying its adversary into jumping the wall. A third bull entered, an especially large cream-colored steer, and faced off against the eight men left in the ring. At this point,

---

* Pope Pius IX had died two years previously, in 1878.

stated one reporter in attendance, "in just twenty seconds by the watch the steer had the ring to himself, and the Spaniards were on the other side of the fence."

The crowd had begun to boo and hiss as another bull was let into the ground. Unfortunately, the creature snagged a cloak with its horn and inadvertently blindfolded itself. In a panic it ran in circles and then charged headfirst into the boards. This was the final straw for Bergh, who requested Superintendent Hartfield of the NYPD to call a halt to the proceedings. There was no need, though. The crowd had lost interest and were already leaving their seats.

The disappointment of all in attendance, who had hoped for the excitement of an authentic *corrida de toros*, was best summarized by a *Herald* reporter the next day, who wrote: "Driving a frightened steer into a ring and then daubing him all over with bunches of ribbons fastened to adhesive plasters is not an exhilarating sight, even when the two-legged performers prance about in tinsel dresses."

OCTOPUS-WRESTLING

One October afternoon in 2012, two American teenagers emerged from the Pacific Ocean with a fresh catch. Ordinarily this wouldn't have drawn a crowd, but in this instance the young divers were wrestling with a nine-foot giant Pacific octopus, and repeatedly punching it in the face.

Earlier that day nineteen-year-old Dylan Mayer had bought a permit from his local Walmart store that legally allowed him to catch and cook an octopus in the local bay area. He had never tried to catch the creature before, but he had experience in bull castration and slaughter, and, assuming these to be transferable skills, he set off with a friend to Alki Beach, West Seattle. Arriving midafternoon, the pair slipped into their wetsuits, checked their regulators, and headed for Cove 2.

Eighty-five feet down amid the wreckage of an old marina he spotted his quarry, and drew his companion's attention. Mayer decided he could take on the slumbering beast single-handedly and grabbed a protruding tentacle. The octopus slipped out of his grasp and retreated further into its nook. The teenager was determined, though, and tugged appendages until he provoked the creature into a furious, whirling attack. Its tentacles wrapped around the boy like a boa constrictor, knocking the breathing apparatus from his mouth as it attempted to squeeze the air from his chest. Mayer managed to replace his regulator, and so began a wrestling match that lasted for over twenty minutes until finally the boys made it to shore.

As they hauled their booty up the beach, a group of furious divers surrounded them, taking pictures and threatening to report them to the authorities. "I caught it, and then these divers came up and started yelling at me," Mayer told KOMO News afterwards. "I ignored them and ended up driving away." Pictures of Mayer triumphantly wielding his trophy began to circulate on the internet to general outrage. The teenager was vilified. Local dive shops banned him, and he received death threats from people who had tracked him down via the web.

Despite the furor, however, his actions were perfectly legal. The law stated that a diver could perform one "harvest" per day, "by hand or by instrument which will not penetrate or mutilate the body." Mayer couldn't understand the anger. "I eat it for meat. It's no different than fishing." A diver from the beach named Bob Bailey told the *Daily Mail* that the teenager had missed the point. "Duck hunting is legal," he said. "It's perfectly legal. But imagine how you would feel if, while you were enjoying these ducks in the park, someone walked up and shot them."

In fact, as misjudged as his choice of time and place were, not only were Mayer's actions legal but they were in fact a renaissance of a once-celebrated sport of the West Coast of America that dates back decades before Mayer was born. In an article for the April 1949 issue of *Mechanix Illustrated*, entitled "Octopus Wrestling Is My Hobby," diver Wilmon Menard described the drama of the sport in magnificent color, declaring the octopus a "demon of fury" and an all-round bugger to kill:

> There would be a human-like moan and the water would be clouded with sepia. The long tentacles would flay the surface of the lagoon in savage fury, as the monster tried to rid itself of our spears which were firmly imbedded in its head. If necessary, another spear would be dispatched into the writhing hulk. It took a long time to tire the octopus and we had to hold firmly to the ropes attached to the end of the spears to prevent it from sinking to the bottom of the lagoon where it would be lost to us.

The article opened up the sport to a whole new audience. "I realize it all sounds like a loathsome sport," wrote Menard, "but it's really more fun than hunting some poor harmless creature. When you wrestle and kill an octopus, you're ridding the marine world of a treacherous enemy."

Popular interest in octopus-wrestling peaked in the 1960s, and contests began to pop up along the coast. In snorkel events lasting two and a half hours, or one-hour scuba hunts, divers would scour rock faces and the ocean floor for the giant cephalopods.

"They have good suction, but if you get their arms and pull, the suction cups go pop, pop, pop. They don't have a lot of holding strength," recalled Gary Keffler, a retired octo-wrestler and competition organizer. In 1963, Puget Sound in Tacoma, Washington, played host to the World Octopus Wrestling Championship. A televised audience watched 111 divers divided into teams drag a total of 25 octopuses from the water, some weighing as much as 26 kilos.

In the 1960s, octopus-wrestling became a popular sport—
so much so that there was even a world championship held in
Puget Sound, Washington, in 1963. (*Getty Images*)

Among fans of the sport was the writer H. Allen Smith, who took the opportunity presented by the resurgent interest to recount the story of one of the originators of the sport in an article for *True* magazine in 1964. In the 1920s, a down-on-his-luck soldier of fortune named Vanderhoeven hit on the idea of harvesting the giant octopuses in residence along the Pacific Coast to sell to the local Chinese community, the members of which considered the meat a delicacy. To pull off the plan, Vanderhoeven teamed up with a former coast guard diver named O'Rourke, whom Smith labeled "the father of octopus wrestling." The two would take a boat out to spots known to be rich in octopus and begin the operation. O'Rourke would strip naked, slip on a diving helmet, and plunge into the water. Vanderhoeven would then winch him down to the ocean floor, puffing on a pipe as the *au naturel* O'Rourke roamed around, searching for prey. The diver had become an expert in teasing the creatures into tying themselves around him, feigning struggle to make them tighten their grasp. At a certain point—usually when he noticed a crunching sound emanating from his constricted bones—O'Rourke signaled Vanderhoeven to pull him up by yanking on the rope, and up the two were hoisted. Once he had successfully dragged O'Rourke's enveloped person back aboard, Vanderhoeven set about the quarry with his *schiavona*, a late seventeenth-century Italian basket-hilted sword he had collected on his travels. The invertebrate's appendages were neatly sliced from around O'Rourke's body one by one and the meat was collected and dried, and then the haul was sold to local merchants and restaurateurs.

When Vanderhoeven and O'Rourke eventually parted ways, O'Rourke took his octo-expertise to Hollywood and became a successful stuntman, advertising himself as an expert at Greco-Roman octopus-wrestling. "It is said," wrote H. Allen Smith years later, "that Cecil B. DeMille admired O'Rourke's work and once engaged him to wrestle an octopus for three days, when he knew quite well he would not be using the episode in the film he was shooting."

ŌLLAMALIZTLI

It's all fun and games until someone loses their head . . . and then it's even more enjoyable. "The Mesoamerican ballgame" is the term used to refer to the sport played by the ancient peoples of Mexico and Central America. In Spanish it's known as *juego de pelota*, in ancient Maya it's *pitz*, and in the language of the Aztecs it was called *Ōllamaliztli*. The ballgame is thought to originate from 1400 BC, and as such we have little in the way of information on how it was played. However, what is apparent is that the game was steeped in ritualistic association. The larger events were often followed by human sacrifices, leading to the commonly held belief that instead of a ball the sport was sometimes played with a freshly decapitated human head. The game may also have served a more practical purpose: some think that it was used as a way to resolve disputes without resorting to combat.

Whether or not it is true that the ancient form of the game was synonymous with human sacrifice, it was certainly violent. The Dominican friar Diego Durán (ca. 1537–1588) witnessed a later version of the match played by Aztecs and described how the players incurred bruises so gruesome that they had to be drained,

An indigenous Mayan takes part in *juego de pelota* in
Guatemala City in 2011. (*Corbis*)

while others were fatally wounded when the ball "hit them in the
mouth or the stomach or the intestines." Contemporary illustrations such as the reliefs at Dainzú and the Teotihuacan murals
indicate that some form of protective gear was worn. Knee pads,
gloves, and elbow pads were incorporated at various stages into
the costume of skirts, capes, and masks; there is even archaeological evidence of a stone yoke costume, though this is thought to be
too impractical to have been worn during the match, and is likely
therefore to have been a form of postgame ceremonial garb.

By combining archaeological evidence with an examination of
the game of *ulama*, a descendant of the original sport that is still
played today, an idea is gleaned of the rules of play: two teams
of between two and four players faced off in the large, brightly

painted stone ballcourts, of which more than 1,300 have been found dating back to the pre-Columbian era. Using their hips mostly, the men would bounce a ball made of rubber (and weighing about four kilos) between them until it left the court or a player failed to keep it in the air. Later versions included the use of rackets and paddles.

The suggestion of human sacrifice comes from the study of the Mayan and Veracruz cultures of a later period, where illustrations on ballcourt walls clearly depict ritual slaughter; the most famous of which is the *jugador de pelota decapitado* (decapitated ballgame player) taken from the Veracruz site of Aparicio and dated to AD 700–900. These Mayan illustrations go some way toward explaining the violent zeal of the contestants, for those executed at the close of the match were in fact players of the ballgame, presumed to be those of the losing side.

Pelota purépecha is an offshoot of the ballgame, played by the Michoacán people of what is now Mexico. In terms of rules and gameplay, the two-thousand-year-old *purépecha* is strikingly similar to modern hockey, except for one significant feature: the ball is on fire. The game is played at night on a stone court, with two teams battling for possession of the fuel-soaked cloth ball, to hit it home into the opposition's goal with *purépecha* that resemble a thin form of the hockey stick. Here again is a sport steeped in symbolism: the flaming ball represents both the sun traveling across the sky and goodness surviving in the darkness of evil. Reflexes and dexterity are crucial: one wrong move and you risk being ignited. The Mexican government has recently invested in demonstrations of the sport to kindle interest in the younger generation and ensure the preservation of an almost-forgotten culture.

OLYMPICS—FORGOTTEN EVENTS

The organization of the first modern Olympic Games was a much more relaxed affair than it is today. There was no rigorous selection process for national teams—the athletes worked it out among themselves, paid an entry fee, and signed up for the events. The program of competitions was drawn up by the host country, not the International Olympic Committee, and as such varied considerably each time. This, of course, resulted in a fair amount of chaos. In 1900, for example, it was only the French players who turned up to compete in the croquet competition. Even stranger, the game was attended by a single spectator: an Englishman, who had made the trip specially from Nice. The staging of competitions on Sundays also caused huge problems: the American long jumper Myer Prinstein was forbidden by his university, Syracuse, from competing on the Sabbath. He struck a deal with his fellow finalist and compatriot, Alvin Kraenzlein, that neither would compete. Kraenzlein, however, reneged on the agreement and went on to beat Prinstein's distance by a mere centimeter, earning him a winner's medal and, later, a punch in the face from his colleague.

In fact, the program of events in the 1900 Summer Olympics in Paris in particular (today officially referred to as the Games of the II Olympiad) is a fascinating jumble of bizarre tournaments, as organizers experimented with the formula. Many events are unique to the 1900 competition: live pigeon shooting, for one. The birds were released from traps before a row of professional gunners, who had each paid two hundred francs for the privilege of blasting as many of the birds out of the sky as possible. In

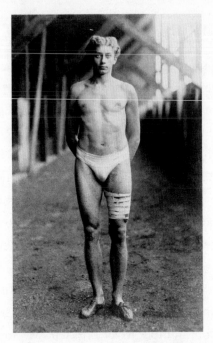

Alvin Kraenzlein demonstrated some behavior that fell
short of the Olympic ideal when he took the winner's
medal in the 1900 Olympics. (*Corbis*)

total, more than three hundred were dispatched, with the prize
of twenty thousand francs sportingly divided by those finishing
in the top four.

The swimming obstacle race was another peculiarity. Held in
the River Seine, the competitors in this two-hundred-meter event
had to clear three sets of aquatic hurdles: dragging themselves
first over a pole and then a row of boats, then diving under a
second row of boats. The Australian Frederick Lane came first
with a time of 2:38.4, narrowly beating Otto Wahle of Austria,
who would later go on to coach the American national swimming
team. Tug-of-war was also played (and continued to be an event

until 1920), with two teams, or "clubs," of six or more members attempting to pull each other across a central dividing line. Sometimes it happened that the clubs were composed of more than one country, as was the case in 1900 when Denmark and Sweden teamed up to claim victory over the French.

As well as these, the five-month-long 1900 Olympiad also included hot air balloon contests, in which the contestants were required to drop a weighted missile on a ground target; the competitive lifesaving event; motor racing; pigeon racing; kite flying; Basque pelota; cricket; equestrian long jump; and others. There was even a firefighting event, divided into contests for volunteer and professional crews. The team from Porto, Portugal, won the volunteer event, with the British team from Leyton coming in second and the team from Budapest third. The professional firefighting fixture was won by an American team from Kansas City, with its "famous engine and hook and ladder company No. 1." The Milanese group were runners-up.

The festival of 1900 is just one example of experimentation with the Olympic program, which, throughout the history of the modern Games, has seen some bizarre inclusions. Here are a few of the more unusual obsolete Olympic events:

American football (1932)
Art competitions (works of architecture, literature, music, painting, and sculpture inspired by sport, 1912–1948)
Australian football (1956)
Bowling (1988)
Budō (Japanese martial art, 1964)
La Canne (French martial art with cane, 1924)

Cycle polo (1908)

Friesian handball (1928)

Gaelic football (1904)

Gliding (1936)

Glima (Viking wrestling, 1912)

Hurling (1904)

Korfball (1920, 1928)

Pesäpallo (Finnish baseball, 1952)

Plunge for distance (1904)

Roller hockey (1992)

Roque (American croquet—in fact, the Americans were the
   only nation to send a team; 1904)

Savate (French kickboxing, 1924)

Waterskiing (1972)

ONE-LEGGED CRICKET

There have been a variety of bizarre cricket matches over the
years. A game was played in September 1762 by two naked
Westminster butchers, who placed the stumps on either side of
a pond that served as the wicket. Married vs. Single was a popular theme, with matches recorded in 1773 and later in 1871 and
1892. Smokers vs. Nonsmokers took place in 1840, summarized
by Henry Colburn later that year in *Calendar of Amusements* with:
"The amusement seems to be intended to be felt, for it is entirely
out of the question to derive any of it through the medium of
sight." In the bitter winter of 1776, a game was even attempted on

ice skates, on the frozen river between New Stairs and Gillingham Reach in Kent.

But perhaps the most striking cricketing spectacle took place in 1796, when a match at the new ground in Montpelier Gardens, London, drew a crowd of such enthusiasm as to result in a riot. The teams were composed of resident pensioners of Greenwich Hospital, which was at the time dedicated to the care of wounded sailors of the Royal Navy. Eleven one-legged men faced eleven one-armed men, to play for a purse of a thousand guineas. The team of one-legged men battled first, and was eventually bowled out for a total of 93; their high scorer, Fearn, chalked up 30 runs not out. The "Greenwich Pensioners with One Arm," as they are listed in the official score book, then took to bat. Though they were able to outpace their monopedal challengers, when it came to swinging a wooden bat the advantage of two hands proved just too great, and the one-armed team was bowled out for 41, with Fearn recorded as taking six of the wickets. A *London Evening Post* reporter wrote that the event "afforded the most excellent sport" to those spectating, many of whom were betting heavily on the result. So great was the appeal, in fact, that the crowd of those unable to gain entry to the ground swelled throughout the day, and when they surged forward to catch a glimpse of the one-legged innings, "the gates were forced open, and several parts of the fencing were broke down, and a great number of persons having got upon the roof of a stable, the roof broke in, and several persons falling among the horses were taken out much bruised."

The match resumed the next morning, and after another destructive bowling session by Fearn the pensioners with one leg

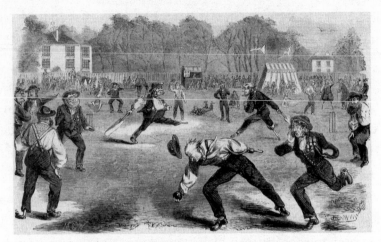

The One Arm and One Leg Cricket Match at Lord's.
Illustrated Sporting News, August 25, 1866.

were announced the winners by 103 runs. A rematch was played the following Wednesday, but victory again went to the one-legged team, who followed it up with a hundred-yard dash for good measure. The first three to hop across the finish line divided the prize money between them.

PEDESTRIANISM

Pedestrianism was competitive endurance walking, popular in the eighteenth and nineteenth centuries. The British sport was heavily gambled upon and its stars were national celebrities, among whom was Foster Powell (1734–1793), an attorney's clerk who set the sport of pedestrianism in motion in 1764 when he walked fifty miles on the Bath Road in seven hours. He embarked on a career as a pedestrian and walked several timed races from

London to York and back, a journey of 396 miles that he completed in 140 hours. Despite being lauded as an endurance sport hero, Powell made only a modest profit from his achievements: the £10 he made from the walk to York was said to be the largest sum he saw.

In contrast, Robert Barclay Allardice (1779–1854) turned the event into a lucrative spectacle when he successfully wagered James Wedderburn-Webster a thousand guineas that he could walk a thousand miles in a thousand hours at Newmarket Heath. As word spread of his attempt, people came from all over the country to watch, and the accommodation in the entire Cambridge area was booked out for weeks. Captain Barclay, as he was known, possessed phenomenal endurance and strength (he was able to lift an eighteen-stone man onto a table using one hand) and advised pedestrians-in-training to cleanse the system by regularly drinking phosphate of soda and then engaging in a daily routine of a half-mile run to warm up, followed by a six-mile walk and a breakfast of rare beef or mutton chops with stale bread and beer. Then another six-mile walk with no break for lunch, followed by a thirty-minute nap and then a brisk four-mile walk and a dinner identical in menu to breakfast. Finally, one should end the day with a half-mile sprint and another six-mile walk before heading to bed at eight o'clock. Perhaps Captain Barclay's strangest advice was to sweat profusely: he recommended that once a week the pedestrian-in-training should dress in thick clothes, sprint for four miles, and then immediately down a pint of a custom concoction he referred to as "sweating liquor," which was composed of "one ounce of caraway-seeds; half an ounce of sugar candy; mixed with two bottles of cider, and boiled down to one half."

Perhaps surprisingly, there was a decent crowd watching this six-day event at the Agricultural Hall, Islington, as seen in the *Graphic*, 1878.

In America, Edward Payson Weston (1839–1929), one of the greatest pedestrians of all, got his start in 1861 when he walked 450 miles from Boston to Washington, DC, to pay off an election bet he had made against Abraham Lincoln. Though Weston arrived too late to see the president being sworn in, he was still able to attend the inauguration ball that evening. Over his pedestrianism career, Weston endured all manner of weather, beatings, and blisters the size of golf balls to cover extraordinary distances: 1,200 miles in 1867 from Portland to Chicago; 1,058 miles across freezing New England; and, in 1909, a (literally) staggering 4,000 miles in 100 days, from New York to San Francisco.

By the turn of the twentieth century, pedestrianism was evolving into professional racewalking, but the spirit was still very much alive among amateurs. In 1911 the title of "Centurion" was introduced in Britain, awarded to those amateur athletes who completed a one-hundred-mile walk within twenty-four hours, a group that became known as the Brotherhood of Centurions, which still exists today; in fact, Centurion clubs can also be found in the United States, Malaysia, the Netherlands, Australia, and New Zealand.

PEOPLE-THROWING

The eighteenth-century German magician Philip Breslaw was famous for being one of the earliest conjurors to feature mind reading in his act. He toured England relentlessly for more than forty years with his signature tricks, such as making eggs jump out of pockets and suspending objects in midair. It is also likely that he was something of a pervert. At one show in Cambridge his misbehavior resulted in him being bodily removed from the theater and suffering an undignified punishment. A member of the audience wrote in a letter dated November 9, 1771:

Last night we had a new exhibition: One Breslau, who shows sleight of hand, came here, and in his performances he gave a piece of paper to three ladies to read, the only three in the room. As soon as they looked at it, they rose; and without speaking, left the place. The gentlemen of the University, immediately guessing that there must be something very gross in what was given them to read, in revenge of the insult tossed the conjurer in a blanket.

The game of throwing someone into the air with a blanket has had a rather strange evolution. In living memory, it serves as a way of celebrating the birthday of the person being tossed; in the eighteenth century, it was a form of penalty; and in the sixteenth century, it was an entertainment with a nastier element since forgotten. In Spanish it's known as *pelele* and in German *prellen*, but it is the Old French word *berne*, meaning winnowing, or separating the chaff from the grain, that gives the clue as to how it was originally played. The person to be thrown lay down on a broad sheet, the edges of which were gripped by a large group of men, typically sixteen in number. Onto the sheet was then poured a sackful of heavy, blunt objects such as work tools, logs, and stones, and the *berne* began. As the victim was thrown up and down, he

A copper engraving from 1573 showing people-throwing by the butchers' guild of Zwickau.

was shaken together with the objects, symbolically separated from the chaff, while often literally separated from consciousness. The tossing drew to a close only when the men grew tired. Just as with fox tossing, the game is linked to the ancient superstitious ritual of warding off evil spirits by throwing a dog or fox into the air with a blanket until it was dead.

Perhaps the most famous recipient of a *berne* is Sancho Panza, in Miguel de Cervantes's *Don Quixote*. In chapter XVII, after he and his master refuse to settle their bill with an innkeeper, Sancho is grabbed by a group of lodgers: "Putting Sancho in the middle of the blanket, they began to raise him high, making sport with him as they would with a dog at Shrovetide."

Elsewhere in the world, the Iñupiat people of northern Alaska celebrate their spring whaling festival, Nalukataq, with a blanket toss. The blanket, which is stitched together from the skins of bearded seals, is then covered in sweets. This custom comes from a more practical origin than that of the *berne*: a hunter would be thrown into the air by the rest of his party to allow him to scan the horizon for quarry. In Corsica, the activity was reported by Dr. Johann August Unzer (1727–1799), editor of the medical weekly *Der Arzt, Eine medicinische Wochenschrift*. The physician claimed that when a married Corsican man died, it was an island custom for all the local women to gather in the house of the deceased and beat the widow for allowing her husband to expire. The corpse was then placed on a blanket and thrown into the air by the women for hours on end, for the tossing occasionally "recalled to life" the man, "who to all appearance had been dead." His desperate bid for freedom foiled, the women left him to the mercy of his former widow.

PHONE BOOTH STUFFING

In the 1950s a group of students in Durban, South Africa, claimed to have set a world record for how many people could be fitted into one telephone booth: twenty-five. This was news to the rest of world, who hadn't been aware that this was a category in which one *could* set a record. The challenge was instantly taken up, and "telephone box squashings," as they were known in England, or "phone booth stuffings" in America, started popping up at student campuses everywhere.

The rules were simple: a person was counted if his or her body was at least halfway inside the booth. The door could be left open and the bodies could be piled in whichever way was preferred, but most attempts adopted the tried-and-tested "sardine" formation. (In England, the attempt was considered successful only if someone inside was also able to answer or make a call, but stuffers in other countries disregarded this stipulation.)

The South African record of twenty-five turned out to be a formidable one to beat. First, at UCLA, a record of seventeen was made. A group of London university students then managed nineteen; seven students in Fresno, California, set their own record by fitting seven boys inside a booth underwater; this was swiftly beaten by a group of their female contemporaries, who squeezed eight coeds into a submerged booth in the Fresno Hacienda Motel pool. In Canada, Ryerson Tech students claimed to have had great success with their custom "sandwich" style of cramming, but it was the stuffing team at St. Mary's College in Moraga, California, who came closest to beating the South Africans' record, wedging twenty-two students inside a seven-foot booth in 1959 with their

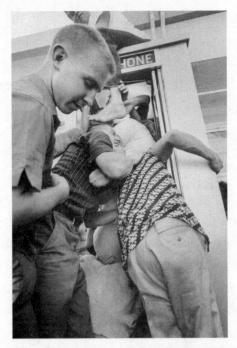

In 1959 at UCLA, phone booth stuffing became
the latest craze. (*Getty Images*)

"crosshatching" technique. The event was photographed for *Life* magazine, and even featured briefly in the opening credits for the television show *Happy Days*.

The interior of the common campus phone booth was soon considered satisfactorily explored, and other forms of cramming started to hit the headlines. In the same year, a group of Alpha Delta Pi and Delta Zeta sorority sisters packed themselves into a Renault to set a record of twenty-seven girls in a car, while male students found an alternative venue: thirty-seven South Dakota State College scholars jammed themselves into an outhouse, with extra space created by leaving the magazine outside on the roof.

As a new academic year started, the fad of stuffing was left behind; except at St. Mary's College, where every few years another attempt is made in celebration of the anniversary of the original effort, with the surviving members of the 1959 team looking on and taunting the new generation of stuffers.

PHOSPHORESCENT GOLF

Professor Alexander Crum Brown (1838–1922) was a respected lecturer in chemistry at the University of Edinburgh and a fellow of the Royal College of Physicians, whose hand once caught fire during a game of golf.

The idea to invent the sport of night golf was that of Brown's colleague, Peter Tait, a professor of natural philosophy and a golfing fanatic who sometimes played as many as five rounds a day. One night in St. Andrews in 1871, Tait proposed to a group of dinner guests—consisting of Brown, the renowned scientist Thomas Henry Huxley, Mrs. Tait, and another invitee—his idea of playing a nocturnal game of golf uninhibited by darkness. His solution was to coat the balls in a phosphorescent paint of his own devising that would make them impossible to lose. Drawn to the humor of the proposal, the group consented to a match and went out into the night to play a round on a nearby course.

According to John L. Low, a famous golfer of the time and friend of Tait's, the invention worked. At least, initially: "The idea is a success; the balls glisten and advertise their situation; the players make strokes which surprise their opponents and apprise themselves of hitherto unknown powers."

The game was drawing to a close as Professor Brown sank his ball on the ninth green and collected it from the hole. At this point, a key lesson was learned in Tait's experiment. Smelling smoke, Brown looked down to find his golfing glove in flames, having reacted with the chemical that coated the ball and spontaneously combusted. The fire was quickly extinguished, and the chastened group returned to their lodging to attend to Brown's scorched hand.

An alternative form of night golf was played in 1906 by two American professionals who competed for a prize of $50 on a North Carolina course using only moonlight to guide their game. A crowd of two hundred people turned out to "watch" Donald Ross beat Jack Jolly 88–93 over two hours, each player aided by an extra caddy who was positioned near the hole to listen for the shot landing. Not a single ball was lost.

PIG-RUNNING

As with cocks, throughout history pigs were commonly used as scapegoats, and spectacles involving their suffering functioned as a kind of superstitious catharsis. From the fifteenth to the eighteenth centuries, medieval Europe saw the popularity of judicial animal prosecutions, in which beasts and insects were put on trial for a variety of crimes in the same superstitious fervor that brought about the witch hunts. Upon conviction (usually the outcome, for the animals were rarely able to mount a cogent defense), they were excommunicated from the Church or, more commonly, hanged. The vast majority of the defendants in these cases were pigs. One of the earliest examples of these proceedings took place in 1386 in Falaise, France, where a court convicted a pig of murdering an infant. The sow was hanged by the neck till dead, but her six piglets, who stood accused of collusion, were pardoned "on account of their youth and their mother's bad example."

Of course, the main arena for porcine abuse was the sports field. A French manuscript of 1425 describes one game played at festivals called *Le jeu de la truie et des quatre aveugles* ("the game of the sow and the four blind men"). A pig was herded into a narrow fenced-off area in which four blindfolded men with clubs were waiting. To the delight of the crowd, the men attempted

"The Game of The Sow and The Blind Men" as
illustrated in *Sports et Jeux d'Adresse.*

to beat the animal to death, though because of their blindfolds they struck each other as often as they did the pig. The city of Lübeck, Germany, staged a similar event in 1386 (clearly not a good year to be a pig), but in a much larger area and with twelve genuinely blind men beating the screaming creature. After several of the men collapsed in exhaustion from swinging in vain, a bell was hung around the neck of the sow and the game continued.

"Pig-running," or "hunting the pig," was a game popular at English fairs and celebrations. The chosen pig had its tail docked and was slathered in soap or grease. The crowd would then chase after the animal, and whoever managed to catch it and hold it above their head by the stump of its tail using only one hand was the winner and the pig's new owner.

After the brutality of such sports fell from popularity, pigs continued to feature in later forms of public entertainment. One of the most famous of these animals was witnessed by Parson James Woodforde (1740–1803), author of *The Diary of a Country Parson*, in which he records seeing the "learned Pigg" in Norwich in 1785:

> After dinner the Captain and myself, went and saw the learned Pigg at the rampant Horse in St. Stephens . . . It was wonderful to see the sagacity of the Animal. It was a Boar Pigg, very thin, quite black with a magic Collar on his Neck. He would spell any word or Number from the Letters and Figures that were placed before him.

PIG-STICKING

Perhaps, excepting murder (ref. Genesis, chapter 2) pig-sticking is one of the oldest sports in the world." So begins Lord Baden-Powell's celebration of boar hunting, *Pigsticking or Hoghunting* (1889), in which he deftly traces its history back to St. George, with whom he credits its inspiration:

> If he wanted to kill the dragon he could easily have done so without risk to himself by leaving a bit of poisoned pork in its way, but as it was he was a true sportsman and preferred to attack it with a hand to hand weapon and to give himself the further handicap of having to manage a horse which probably hated a monster that breathed fire in its face.

Hunting boar certainly has ancient origins. In Persia, noblemen pursued and cornered the animals using elephants before striking them down with arrows, as documented in the reliefs on the arches of Taq Bostan. Hunting swine with dogs was also common across the Old World, usually with bay-and-catch dogs, which pinned the animal in place and barked until a hunter caught up to finish it off. In ancient Greece, slaying the nocturnal boar was seen as a symbolic act of good triumphing over evil—the hunt for the monstrous Calydonian Boar is one of the great Olympian myths. In medieval Britain, the wild boar that inhabited the forests were as formidable as those found anywhere in the world. In *The Master of Game* (1413), the oldest English-language book on hunting, Edward of Norwich wrote of the creature:

It is the beast of this world that is strongest armed and can sooner slay a man than any other . . . the wild boar slayeth a man with one stroke as with a knife, and therefore he can slay any other beast sooner than they could slay him. It is a proud beast and fierce and perilous, for many times have men seen much harm that he hath done. For some men have seen him slit a man from knee up to the breast and slay him all stark dead at one stroke so that he never spake thereafter.

In nineteenth-century India the boar as quarry had grown in popularity largely out of necessity. The native bear population had dwindled to scarcity thanks to the previous game of choice: bear-sticking. The Indian boar hunts usually took place in the season from February to July. The Bengalese used a short, broad-bladed javelin of considerable weight that was hurled at the pigs and then retrieved. The British cavalry officers introduced a refined spear that never left the hand, and it quickly became the default pig stick. Two versions were used: the long spear was made from bamboo, was eight feet in length and had a steel tip. It was held in one hand about two-thirds of the way from the head, with the knuckles turned down and the thumb along the shaft. The short, or jobbing, spear was heavier. Six and a half feet long, it was easier to wield in jungle, though carried with it a greater risk of the boar reaching the hunter. In fact, the chances of getting "tusked" were significant, and many of the spears were fitted with cross guards to prevent the animal from running itself through along the length of the spear as it desperately tried to gore the hunter.

The pig-sticking would begin with the hunters gathering in

An early illustration of boar hunting, taken from Schwerdt's
famous hunting bibliography (1939).

bushy and marshy areas known to be populated with the beasts.
A team of beaters led by a mounted *shikari* (guide) then drove the
boars from cover, sometimes firing guns into the air and sending
in dogs in a process known as "rearing." As the animals scattered,
the riders charged; being the first to draw blood from a pig was
a coveted honor. Wild boar are phenomenally quick and nimble
creatures, and so the successful pig-sticker had to possess strength,
good aim, and sizable courage (the military were keen to encourage their officers to practice the sport).

"Not only is pig-sticking the most exciting and enjoyable sport
for both the man and horse as well," said Baden-Powell, "but I
really believe that the boar enjoys it too."

The following is some old pig-sticking vocabulary:

Frank	—	a boar enclosure
Jhow	—	a tamarisk, an Old World shrub used as cover by the boar
Jink	—	when the boar changes direction sharply
Nullah	—	a dry watercourse
To pig	—	to hunt the boar
Pug	—	the tracks left by the boar
Pugging	—	tracking the boar
Ride to hog	—	hunting the boar
Rootings	—	marks left in the ground by the boar's snout
Sanglier	—	a boar that has peeled off from the sounder
Sounder	—	a family of wild boar
Squeaker	—	a youngling
Tusker	—	a fully grown boar

PORCUPINE HUNTING

Arm'd at all points, in Nature's guardian mail,
See the stout Porcupine his foes assail;
And, urg'd to fight, the ready weapons throw,
Himself at once the quiver, dart, and bow.
Claudian (ca. AD 370–404)

Hunting porcupines was a rare and curious sport, undertaken in Africa and parts of India more for the novelty than any practical purpose, as the porcupine posed little threat to man or his livestock. It didn't even provide much of a chase, given its reported tendency to scrabble up the nearest tree and wait until its pursuer grew bored. *The Sporting Magazine* of April 1803 does mention, however, that they were a bane to the gardeners of the Cape of Good Hope region, who solved the issue by booby-trapping the vegetable patches, tying carrots and turnips with string to the triggers of loaded shotguns.

One method of hunting was to chase it until it climbed the tree and shoot it down with arrows. Another was to send dogs into its burrow and, when it flees, trap it with blankets, nets, or snares. Captain Thomas Williamson touches on the sport while describing boar hunting in his *Oriental Field Sports* of 1807:

> Porcupines are often found in beating canes for hogs, and are easily speared. With respect to shooting their quills, it is altogether fabulous: dogs are apt to run upon them, and the quills, being sharp, penetrate so deeply, and hold so fast, as to occasion them to quit their matrices or insertions in the porcupine's skin. The wounds are not dangerous, except from their depth. Many horses will not approach porcupines when running, by reason of a peculiar rattling their quills make against each other. The horseman should stab his spear into them without hesitation; there being no danger in approaching them.

During his time in Algeria, the nineteenth-century French explorer Jules Gérard reported local associations of men—labeled *hatcheicheia* because of their fondness for smoking *hashish*—who were devoted to the destruction of the porcupine. The clubs competed as to which could wreak the most damage on the porcupine population. Gérard mentions that he himself "took fabulous numbers of them with small lassos" in Bougie (now Béjaïa) and Guelma, yet was most impressed by the brutal technique of the *hatcheicheia*, who set out into the countryside in groups of ten, taking with them dogs "usually afflicted with the mange," five-foot staffs with serrated metal blades, and a ten-year-old child. When the porcupine burrows were located, the dogs were sent in, followed by the Algerian child, who was wrapped head to toe in protective cloth and yet was still so thin as to "resemble a weasel." The porcupine hunters then waited. Eventually the dogs would burst from the hole followed by the badly bitten boy, who would dump a struggling porcupine of similar size to himself at the feet of the hunters. The men then set upon it with their blades before it could escape. They sliced its throat and then emptied its stom-

An original drawing by Stradanus (1523–1605)
shows how porcupine hunting worked.

ach, filling it with salt and herbs to keep the meat fresh while it was transported back to Constantine.

Indeed, the cooking pot was the final destination of the vast majority of captured porcupines.* "The flesh of the young ones is very good," commented Williamson, "and somewhat similar to pork or veal." *The Sporting Magazine* agreed: "The flesh is said to be excellent eating, and is frequently introduced at the politest tables at the Cape . . . it is the better for hanging a day or two in the chimney."

PUNTGUNNING

In the seventeenth century, when it came to hunting with guns, the prevailing theory was "the larger the barrel, the further the range," and the weapons produced began to reflect this tenet. Matchlock guns increased in size to the point where they became too heavy to carry, and often had to be attached to carriages and dragged to the killing fields by horses. This was before the time when it was considered bad sportsmanship to shoot birds on the ground, and so weapons with a range sufficient to blow apart entire flocks pecking at the soil were of great appeal. The bore diameters were extraordinary, and the barrels ranged in length and reached up to eight feet.

These giant weapons maintained their popularity into the eighteenth century, when they were incorporated into warfare as

---

* But not for all. The eccentric British curio collector Sir Ashton Lever (1729–1788) had a pet porcupine which he would put out to play in his garden with his other pets, a hunting leopard and a giant Newfoundland.

the "wall gun," the "rampart gun," and the "amusette." In a letter to George Washington dated May 19, 1776, General Charles Lee wrote: "I am likewise furnishing myself with four-ounced rifle-amusettes, which will carry an infernal distance; the two-ounced hit a half-sheet of paper 500 yards distant." The big guns also continued to be favored by hunters: Colonel Peter Hawker extolled the virtues of the giant bore in his *Instructions to Young Sportsmen* (first published in 1814), in a chapter strikingly entitled "Wild-fowl Artillery." But perhaps one of the most famous proponents of the big gun was the nineteenth-century game hunter Sir Samuel White Baker. He arrived in northeast Africa brandishing a gun specially commissioned from Holland & Holland, which he had fondly nicknamed "Baby" but which was referred to by his Arab servants as the "cannon's child." There was no doubting Baby's lethal effectiveness, despite a recoil that sent its operator spinning backwards "like a weathercock in a hurricane."

Despite the popularity of guns this size, the issue of mobility, or lack thereof, was a consistent problem: "Let me see the man who will invent anything to work a staunchion-gun over bad ground," wrote Hawker. When the big guns were introduced into the pursuit of waterfowling, however, this hurdle was overcome by the use of small rowing boats, and soon local wildlife populations were devastated by a sport that became known as "puntgunning."

Punt guns were monsters: sometimes weighing more than two hundred pounds, with barrels reaching ten feet in length. At the optimum range of one hundred yards, the shot punched broad holes in entire flocks, leaving waters choked with dead fowl. This was not a sport that championed marksmanship. Any injured quarry were picked off by the gunner with a regular rifle known as a "cripple stopper." A single day's puntgunning could result in a haul of hundreds. Sir Ralph Payne-Gallwey wrote of one such successful expedition off the Dutch coast in October 1889:

> We went afloat today at 12 o'clock and by 3 o'clock I had fired four shots. I killed in these four shots no less than 132 widgeon! Each shot as follows, 33, 14, 40, 45! The third shot was without exception the best one I ever fired into and had I aimed properly I must have bagged 80 to 100 birds!

Puntgunning was usually a two-man operation. The trigger-man lay on his belly in the boat, his feet braced against the sides to absorb the recoil, with the gun resting along the bow. His

A photograph of Snowden Slights with a punt gun from the early twentieth century. (*Yorkshire Museum*)

companion crouched behind him, paddling and steering the boat within range of the unsuspecting flock.

The sport was not without its drawbacks. The low punt boats were at the mercy of the weather, and capsizing was common. In the nineteenth century, when puntgunning was most popular, the gunners increased the powder charges to as much as two pounds, the ignition of which gave the guns a potentially lethal recoil that resulted in many a broken shoulder. Of greater concern, though, was the tendency of the heavily loaded gun to explode in its owner's face. Peter Hawker recorded in his diary in February 1818 that his ninety-six-pound gun burst apart and set him on fire, which he managed to put out before it could reach the pound of gunpowder in his pocket. The obliterative sport was eventually banned in the USA in 1916, and in England the Protection of Birds Act 1954 restricted punt guns to a more modest barrel diameter of 1¾ inches.

THE QUINTAIN

If wealth, sir knight, perchance be thine,
In tournaments you're bound to shine:
Refuse—and all the world will swear
You are not worth a rotten pear.
Thirteenth-century satirical poem

Europe in the High Middle Ages (eleventh to thirteenth centuries) was the time of chivalry, and for knights the grand tournaments were opportunities to exhibit their strength and skill in a series of martial contests. These included the joust, which, like the other events, was accessible only to men of a status above squire. The quintain, however, opened the sport to all. Involving a dummy fixed on a pike driven into the ground, it was a training device with which a man could spar or alternatively charge with a lance. The quintain can be traced back to the Romans, with some historians attributing the invention to Quintas, an inventor about whom little is known. The fourth-century Roman writer Vegetius describes how young military men practiced with the device twice daily, and in the codes of law instituted by the Emperor Justinian, the quintain is referenced as a famous sport.

Originally it was nothing more than a tree trunk at which soldiers hurled spears or beat with clubs. Over time, it developed into a staff bearing a shield, and then a human figure carved from wood to provide a more realistic adversary. The High Middle Ages were also the time of the Crusades, and the dummy was commonly given the likeness of a glaring Turk* or Saracen wielding a club or sword in one hand. (The Italians referred to the sport as "running at the armed man" or "running at the Saracen.")† The whittled torso was placed six feet high on a pivot, and the goal of the horseman was to strike the figure with his lance directly between its eyes—if his weapon should shatter in the process,

---

* There is a story—probably apocryphal—that a Turkish envoy once attended a running at the quintain thrown in his honor. The man watched the display impassively before saying to his hosts: "Didn't it strike you that possibly the Turk would not stand still?"

† Incidentally, the funfair carousels of today originate from a military exercise practiced by the Turks and Arabs at this time, in which they would ride horses in tight circles hurling heavy balls to each other. The Spanish word for this sight was *carosella*, or "little battle."

so much the better. If, however, he missed and clipped the side of the target, the Saracen or Turk would swing around and cuff the rider as he passed, knocking him from his steed and causing him to forfeit the game, as well as suffer the ridicule of those watching. Those without a horse would charge on foot, with a scoring system based on where the quintain was struck and how many blows the attacker got in. The top of the nose between the eyes won three points; the nose below the eyes gained two; the chin, one. Anything else wasn't counted, and if the dummy was turned, the contestant was instantly disqualified and unable to run again for the rest of the day. A fifteenth-century poem entitled "Knyghthode and Batayle" reveals that quintain contestants would use weapons of double the standard weight as a form of strength training.

One of the earliest English quintain contests recorded in detail is mentioned by the Benedictine monk Matthew Paris in *Historia Anglorum* (1250–1259). He describes how a group of young Londoners set up a quintain with a prize of a peacock, which was gate-crashed by the servants of Henry III who were curious about the spectacle. Calling the Londoners "cowardly knaves" and "rascally clowns," the servants were beaten and sent packing, which infuriated the king to such an extent that he fined the city of London a thousand marks. (It was suspected that the provocateurs were sent deliberately, in retaliation for London refusing to join the crusade.)

Sometimes the jouster was carried by a wooden horse, dragged by a team; other times, a "live quintain" event took place. A sparring partner took the place of the dummy and, armed with just a shield, would have to face down charging horsemen and deflect

An illustration of the quintain in use, taken from *Military and religious life in the Middle Ages and at the period of the Renaissance* (1874) by Paul Lacroix.

their lance strikes. Writing of this human quintain, Charles du Fresne (1610–1688) quotes the author of *Le Roman de Giron le courtois* (ca. 1400), who writes of a knight telling another: "I do not by any means esteem you sufficiently valiant for me to take a lance and just [joust] with you; therefore I desire you to retire some distance from me, and then run at me with all your force, and I will be your quintain."

Another popular alternative was the water quintain, also known as "the fisherman's joust," which is mentioned by William Fitzstephen. A pole was fixed in the Thames with a shield or square board attached to the head. A team of rowers propelled a small boat toward it, with a young member of the team standing in the prow of the boat, clutching a lance. The people loved it, and filled bridges, wharves, and riverbanks to watch the competition that also involved boats jousting each other.

The feudal quintain game began to disappear as Europe underwent its bourgeois revolutions, and gradually it slipped from memory, transferring instead to an existence of poetic reference for writers such as Shakespeare, who calls on it for a poignant metaphor in the first act of *As You Like It*. Orlando, suddenly overwhelmed with love for Rosalind, declares:

My better parts
are all thrown down,
And that which here stands up
is but a quintain, a mere lifeless block.

RACING DEER

The black-tailed deer native to western North America had ever served only one sporting purpose—as quarry for hunters—when in 1934 Mr. and Mrs. Wilbur Timm of California bought twenty-eight fawns in Oregon and brought them to their farm in Kelsey, El Dorado County. The Timms had a different plan in mind for the animals: to race them like horses around a steeplechase track.

When the fawns had reached the age of three months, the middle-aged couple began them on a training program that would last a year. The first, and hardest, step, said Mrs. Timm, was to teach the wild animals to become accustomed to wear-

Maybelle and Wilbur Timm with their racing deer in 1935.

ing a collar and leash. This was achieved by tying the deer to a wire fastened between two trees. The animal could enjoy running with a limited amount of freedom while adjusting to the restraint. Because of the high risk of the deer hurting itself while trying to escape, every minute of the process was watched over by the trainers until the taming began to take hold. The next step was to teach the deer to follow the trainer, which involved leading it around by the leash for two days without rest, until it meekly submitted and began to trail the Timms of its own accord. The final stage was teaching it to run the track, which meant introducing the deer to the concept of hurdles. The Timms led them over the obstacles one by one, but encountered a fundamental difference in nature between horse and deer: the latter have no motivation to run or jump unless they are being pursued. The family dog was ordered to give chase, but the deer were easily able to outrun him. And so the training was completed by Mr. Timm, who led the family horse out onto the track, leapt up into the saddle, and charged down the deer, who bolted like streaks of lightning. After repeated races in this fashion they began to get the idea, and when released from their custom-built starting gates they could complete a circuit in thirty-one seconds flat.

The Timms exhibited their racing deer, headed by their star stag, Chief, at various venues around the county in the hope that the sport would take up a regular place alongside greyhound racing. Though it is a story worthy of Walt Disney, with no competitive element (for the deer had little interest in outrunning each other) the enterprise was seen as a gimmick, and failed to ignite further interest.

RATTING

It was the smell that first struck you upon venturing down the rickety wooden stairs: the stench of filthy rats, dogs, and humans, mixed in with a miasma of cigar smoke and cheap beer. You found yourself in a dank basement, filled wall to wall with boisterous gamblers, snarling bulldogs, and wriggling sacks of rats, and if you managed to fight your way ringside you were in prime position to witness a form of animal fighting that, while savage, distinguished itself from other forms of baiting with its focus on speed of kill rather than sustained suffering.

The 1822 Cruel Treatment of Cattle Act, later amended by the Cruelty to Animals Act of 1835, had been introduced to finally put an end to the brutal animal-baitings so common to British towns and cities. Baiting with bulls, dogs, bears, and cocks was on its way out, but there was one kind of animal excluded from the protection of the legislation: vermin. Rat-baiting, in which a sack of rats is emptied into a ring and set upon by a furious dog, had begun as a way for breeders to test the killing aptitude of their young terrier pups. The potential for a spectator (i.e., gambler's) sport was instantly recognized. There were few qualms about the cruelty of the practice, for the rat was a particularly hated figure, seen as a destructive, disease-spreading blight. The ratters were merely providing a public service.

Initially, the number of opponents the dog faced was decided by his size—one for every pound he weighed. The match was presided over by a referee and a timekeeper; the length of time it took one dog to dispatch the rats was noted, and was then contested by a rival canine. The most effective ratters were terriers, the best of whom were those who killed the rat with a swift bite between head and shoulder. The dogs that took the time to bite and then shake the rat, usually the purebred terriers, wasted too many valuable seconds and invariably lost. When the fight was over, the dog was removed from the ring, and the rats thought to be alive were laid out on a table within a marked circle. The referee hit them three times on the tail with a stick. If the rat crawled out of the circle, it was placed back into the ring with the dog, which had the extra time added to his final score.

The most famous of the rat-baiting dogs was Billy, or "Billy the Raticide" as he was also known, grandson of the famous bulldog Turpin, great-grandson of the legendary Blind Turk. He was a bull and terrier, a now extinct breed that was a mix of the original English bulldog (also extinct) and a terrier, bred by the famous James Yardington and owned by Mr. Charles Dew. The breed was rarely used in ratting; terriers were usually favored for their superior speed, but Billy possessed all the speed of the terrier with the added strength and killer instinct of the bulldog, making him a formidable foe. Billy began building a name for himself as a prolific rat killer, with several of his match results surviving on record: in 1820, for example, in a match against Mr. Gill's Jack, he killed twenty rats in two minutes eight seconds. Later in the same year, in competition with Mr. Baker's dog, Tulip, he killed the same number in one minute ten seconds. In 1822 greater challenges were being thrown his way: on September 3, competing against the clock for a wager of twenty sovereigns, Billy finished off one

A drawing of "Billy the Raticide" in Westminster by G. Hunt.

hundred rats in eight minutes forty-five seconds, a new record; but it was a ratting in 1823 that saw him immortalized by an unknown artist with the print *Rat Killing Dog*, when he crushed the life out of 120 rats in eight minutes twenty seconds. After the blood had been washed from Billy's muzzle he was presented with a silver collar and ribbons, and exited to the cheers of an adoring crowd. The dog was a local folk hero, and his raticidal prowess even inspired one fan to dedicate a poem to him:

> *Oh Billy! Let me celebrate thy fame,*
> *Proclaim thy true blood, and exalt thy name.*
> *For, in these vile degenerate times,*
> *Thou shouldst be made conspicious in rhymes.*
> *'Tis mere instinct—antipathy in cats,*
> *But thou, from principle, dost strangle rats . . .*

After his death in 1829, Billy was stuffed and put on display at the Westminster pit. His records stood for years, even as the number of rats thrown into the pits were steadily increased to maintain an interested audience. One spectacular rat-baiting took place on May 1, 1862, when the fearsome bulldog Jacko, regarded as the rightful heir to Billy's mantle of world rat-killing champion, fought in the pit for more than one hundred minutes without a break, in which time he killed one thousand rats (this works out to about one rat every six seconds). It was a new world record, which Jacko surpassed in August 1862, when, in a frenzy, he clocked an astounding average rat-killing time of 2.7 seconds.

As explored in monkey-fighting, it wasn't just dogs that took on the rats in the ring. An extraordinary match took place in August

1823 at the Bainbridge Street cockpit in St. Giles, in which a man killed one hundred rats in six minutes with his bare hands. Before a capacity crowd of gamblers, Mr. William Crafter, superintendent of the granary of the Angel Inn, St. Clement's, performed the feat "in a scene of squeezing and twisting" as one onlooker described the massacre; especially impressive considering he possessed only one good eye. He then "retired without a scratch."

For a long time the Society for the Prevention of Cruelty to Animals was unwilling to attempt to outlaw the rat-baiters: the vermin were hated by the public, and initial bids to ban the sport in defense of the rats were laughed out of court. But by the 1880s the RSPCA was successfully convincing magistrates that the sport was as cruel to the dogs as it was to the rodents, as well as being corrosive to the moral character of the nation.

THE ROYAL GAME

In 1897 there appeared a game played by cyclists known as "the royal game," which defied all predictions of popularity by sinking without a trace soon after. It was a kind of polo played on a bicycle, but instead of a ball the riders used sticks to drive a "play-wheel," a twenty-eight-inch wheel with a pneumatic tire four and a half inches wide. This initial concept would surely have been sufficient to ensure a good contest, but the royal game was conceived with further intricate detail. The field in which the two teams of nine riders rode around was divided into two halves by a chalk line. An alleyway (and here is where the snag in the design becomes apparent) constructed with tightly strung cables extended through the center of the pitch, down which the play-wheel was rolled by the players, who pedaled in circuits around the perimeter. The idea was to roll the wheel through the central alleyway and into one of the goals at each end of the ground. The players had to cycle always in single file, and always in opposite directions, which meant they constantly encountered each other as they lapped the course. The *Los Angeles Herald* in 1897 described the game as "requiring swift riding and much skill and a novice would scarcely venture to form one of a team." The high risk of collision and of garrotting oneself on the high-tension cables was exciting, certainly, but ultimately the wearisome frequency of injury and having to stop and pick up the wheel each time it fell on its side sealed the fate of the royal game.

SKI BALLET

At the Calgary Winter Olympics of 1988, three new forms of skiing made their official debut as demonstration sports. Collectively known as freestyle skiing, the three events for men and women were moguls, aerials, and ballet. The mogul event (skiing downhill over mounds) went on to become an official medal event at the 1992 Albertville Games, as did the aerial (jumps) event at Lillehammer in 1994. Ski ballet, however, was never invited to the Olympic table. It enjoyed a burst of popularity before the International Ski Federation consigned it to obscurity, ceasing all formal competition of the sport after 2000.

The origin of freestyle skiing as a whole goes back to the early twentieth century. European skiers had begun experimenting with daring maneuvers, incorporating somersaults into their displays to impress the public. By the 1920s skiers in the United States had caught the bug and added acrobatic techniques such as flipping, spinning, and jumps to their training. Then, in 1929, an Austrian named Fritz Reuel wrote *New Possibilities in Skiing*, proposing a new form of skiing incorporating formal stunts akin to those of figure skating, with illustrations of the techniques. One such maneuver involved the skier turning on the inside ski while raising the other into the air behind him. It was christened "the Reuel" and went on to become a key ski ballet move known as the "Royal Christie." Doug Pfeiffer's School of Exotic Skiing (1956–62) developed Dr. Reuel's ideas with new tricks such as the mambo, the Charleston, spinners, tip rolls, and crossovers.

Freestyle's relaxed approach to downhill skiing had become known as "hot-dogging" and hit its stride in the 1960s when advances in ski equipment allowed a new, more freely expressive generation to experiment on the slopes. "You get ripped away from controls, from society, from washing your clothes, from taxes, from cutting your hair," said Mike Lund, a freestyle skier interviewed at the time, who had run away from home at age fifteen to later join the Sun Valley ski patrol.*

The introduction of short skis rendered tricks easier to perform, and equipment manufacturers quickly began creating tai-

---

* Incidentally, this quote is taken from *The Story of Modern Skiing* by John Fry, who also notes that Lund was later wanted in 1978 in connection with the smuggling of a shipment of Colombian marijuana valued at several million dollars, but eluded police for more than twenty years by living under the name "Lance McCain."

lored skis designed for each of the freestyle events. Particularly popular were the K2 Bermuda Shorts, mainly because of the name. Ski ballet now came into its own.

Sometimes referred to as "snow dancing" and later rebranded "acroski" in an effort to add some machismo, ski ballet incorporated moves from figure skating, classical ballet, and gymnastics, with the skier performing a ninety-second routine set to music on a gentle slope. The choreography featured jumps, pole flips, rolls, leg-crossings, pole-twirling, and spins while skiing, with the dancers all the while emoting to the strains of Chopin, Mozart, and Huey Lewis and the News. Routines were judged by a panel and marked on technical difficulty, composition, and style.

Proponents of the sport praised the benefits of developed balance, fitness, flexibility; spectators just loved the show. At its peak popularity, ski ballet competitions possessed all the pageantry and drama of the ice dance, with crowds dazzled by sensational costumes: competitors roamed the slopes in capes, headbands, shoulder pads, matador costumes, sequins, puffy sleeves, spandex, and glitter gloves. If these failed to capture the crowd's attention, then the smoke bombs, light shows, confetti, and even jazz bands sure didn't. Television producers took note, and the ballet skiers found themselves performing for millions of viewers. Audiences loved the vibrancy, the flashiness, and the sight of athletes somersaulting over their ski poles. A new lexicon entered the public discourse, with stunt names like the Back Scratcher, the Wheelie, the Mule Kick, the Iron Cross, the Revolution Jump, and the Tip Drag and terms such as Burned Out of the Scenery (crashing in competition) and the Gay Gainer (two men flipping while they hold hands) discussed around the world. In the 1980s the ski ballet pas de deux competition was introduced, in which a couple performed the usual spins, jumps, and leg-crossing but also lifts in a synchronized routine.

Several key figures emerged from the scene. Suzanne "Suzy ChapStick" Chaffee, a former Ford model and Olympic alpine skier, became the face of ballet skiing in the early 1970s, a preeminence that won her a long-running television campaign advertising ChapStick lip balm from which she gained her inescapable sobriquet. Possessing both beauty and a phenomenal litheness perfectly suited to the sport, Chaffee had taken up freestyle skiing after finishing twenty-eighth in the downhill event at the 1968 Winter Olympics in Grenoble, a result she attributed to apply-

Suzy "ChapStick" Chaffee displays some of the extraordinary flexibility that made her a star of ski ballet. (*Getty Images*)

ing the wrong kind of wax to her skis. Despite the ignomini-
ous placing, her skintight chrome racing suit caught the world's
attention, and when she turned her sights on the freestyle event,
the spotlight followed. "ChapStick" Chaffee was crowned world
freestyle ski champion three times between 1971 and 1973 in
competitions against both men and women, for at the time there
was no women's division. Her trademark moves, which included
the eye-watering Suzy Split—in which she performed a complete
forward split while balanced on the tips of her skis—ensured her
legendary status. She later became the first woman invited to join
the US Olympic Committee and the eligibility committee, and
went on to form the World Sports Foundation with Bill Bradley,
Jack Kelly, and Muhammad Ali.

Thanks to ChapStick Chaffee the sport had been infused with
an added dose of glamour, but it was the emergence of another
figure that brought a new entertainment value. In 1975 "The
Puppet" appeared and began to dominate competitions. Dressed
in black with his face covered in a thick layer of clown makeup,
Alan Schoenberger, a former dancer and professional mime, had
finally found his perfect performance medium.

Schoenberger, who never revealed his age "for theatrical reasons," initially got off to a rocky start with ski ballet, suffering a
separated shoulder, broken ribs, a punctured lung, and biting his
tongue almost in two. "My doctor told me to stop competing or
I would probably die," he later said. However, in 1975, after a
summer of training on a self-designed machine made from rolling
pins, he entered the first competition of the season at Stowe, Ver-
mont, and performed a ski routine to Bach's Minuet in G major,
which was broadcast live by ABC. He decided to focus solely on

ski ballet, shaved off his mime's mustache, and the next year he won the Ski Ballet World Championships.

However, after a whirlwind year of global travel, parties, and press attention, Schoenberger grew frustrated with the increasing amount of regulation constricting the sport and began to act up. While getting high with an Italian snowcat driver, he convinced the man to hand over the controls and took off down a course prepared for the following day, obliterating the hay bale

Annika Johansson of Sweden shows what ski ballet was all about back in 1992. (*Getty Images*)

jumps. When he was penalized for not using ski poles in his performances, he improvised an elaborate routine mocking the decision. Then, in the last stage of the final competition of the 1977 season, as he was poised to claim the world title for the second time, he decided midway through his routine that he had had enough. He gestured to the soundman to switch off the music, stepped out of his skis, and simply walked away. "It was seen as an aggressive move," he recalls, "but I wanted to make the statement that even though I got competitive on the ballet circuit, I was only really there because I wanted to dance."

Soon after, the increasing regulation and widespread banning of the more acrobatic elements of ski ballet began to bring about its demise. Costumes were phased out, and public interest began to fade. "They stripped the heart out of it," said Schoenberger. Despite its inclusion as a demonstration sport at the 1988 and 1992 Olympics, ski ballet never gained the official recognition its supporters felt it deserved. The sport quickly faded away, leaving the world to check its drink and wonder whether the whole thing had been some kind of drug-induced hallucination.

STILTS VS. RUNNERS VS. HORSES

In the nineteenth century the Landes region of Gascony, France, consisted of great plains of marshes, bogs, and wet sands, with few roads and a scattered population of sheep farmers. To navigate this difficult terrain the shepherds used stilts. Called *tchangues*, meaning "long legs," the poles were five feet long and featured stirrups and leg straps for support. The men also carried a long staff with which they steadied themselves as they moved and herded their sheep. When it came time to take a break, the staff was used to form a tripod so that they could rest upright, while they knitted or spun on a distaff that they carried in their belt, next to the gun used against wolves. The added height also afforded another advantage for the stilt-walking shepherds of Landes: they were able to see for great distances, allowing them to keep track of their flocks and spot predators. The Landais learned the skill in childhood and were a source of national pride: when Empress Josephine met Napoleon in Bayonne in 1808, a group of stiltsmen were sent to escort her, easily keeping up with the horse-drawn carriage. During her stay, they entertained her by running races and performing stunts.

As the century aged, the practice gradually began to disappear, but a baker from Arcachon named Sylvain Dornon was determined to preserve the culture of the Landes stilt-walkers and staged a series of races to show they could be used for sport. In 1889 he and his group of stiltsmen made a presentation to a large crowd in the park of the Moorish Casino of Arcachon. The men raced each other over short distances and played the fife and *tchalamine* (a kind of folk oboe) while dancing on their poles. Later that year, during the world's fair, Dornon brought further publicity to his cause by climbing the Eiffel Tower on his stilts. He returned to Arcachon inspired by his success in Paris, and it was then that he hatched the plan that would bring him worldwide fame.

Dornon decided to attend the Franco-Russian Exhibition that was due to be staged in Moscow in May 1891 by walking the entire distance from France to Russia on stilts. The maga-

The inhabitants of Landes relied on stilts because of the boggy nature of the region, as seen in Henry René d'Allemagne's 1903 book.

zine *L'Illustration* agreed to fund the trip and, on March 12, two thousand people filled the Place de la Concorde to see Dornon, mounted on stilts and in full shepherd's garb, begin the journey. Over every variety of terrain, most of which was off-road, Dornon maintained a daily coverage of sixty kilometers with an itinerary that took in Reims, Sedan, Luxembourg, Coblentz, Berlin, Wilna (Vilnius), and finally, after fifty-eight days of walking, Moscow on May 10. A police escort led him to the exhibition as crowds cheered and shouted *"Vive la France!"*

Dornon's adventures inspired others in the Landes region and, in the early 1890s, there was a flurry of racing on stilts, usually performed as a celebration on Ascension Day. The race to beat all races, though, took place in May 1894 in Bastide, a suburb of Bordeaux. In a contest like no other before or since, it was decided to test the stiltsmen's speed by pitting three of them against three racers on foot and three racers on horseback over a course of 250 miles on a route that would take them through Libourne, Bergerac, Mussidan, Périgueux, Angoulême, Cognac, Saintes, Blaye, and Bordeaux.

On May 3, at twenty minutes to ten, the race began: the horses took an immediate and considerable lead, followed by the pedestrians, and then the stiltsmen. Some fifty-five miles into the race the stiltsmen had overtaken the pedestrians, one of whom had dropped out. At Angoulême, 141 miles in, two of the horses (one drawing a buggy) and three stiltsmen remained in the race, the men on foot having been left far behind. At Jarnac (160 miles) the two horsemen arrived and took a rest. The first stiltsman to arrive immediately started off again, leaving the horses behind, and was the first to register at Saintes (180 miles) after forty-four hours and forty-four minutes of travel. The ridden horse, Charlatan, caught up with him, and in the final stretch the race was neck and neck, until finally the horse pulled ahead and claimed victory. The contestants were checked by a doctor and found to be in perfect health. The exhausted horse was put away, while the stiltwalker indulged in only a brief respite before inquiring about the possibility of a rematch.

STOOLBALL

Before cricket, baseball, and rounders were so much as glimmers in sporting eyes, there was stoolball, a sport that dates back to 1450 (possibly even earlier), originating in Sussex in the south of England. Just as with other rural games, such as last couple in hell and hot cockles, stoolball, which was sometimes referred to as "cricket in the air," involves the participation of both men and women, and has a long association as a game of courtship: in Fletcher and Shakespeare's comedy *Two Noble Kinsmen* from 1634, for example, the suggestion of playing stoolball is used as innuendo between a female character and her wooer:

> Daughter: Will you goe with me?
> Wooer: What shall we doe there, wench?
> Daughter: Why, play at stoole ball:
> What is there else to doe?

There is some debate as to how the game was officially played, as it is not known for certain whether it was separate from a sport called "stobball" or whether they were one and the same. However, as it is commonly understood, stools or tree stumps were used in the same way as wickets are in cricket and bases are in baseball. Originally played by milkmaids and their suitors, a player (usually the maid) would sit on a stool and attempt to defend it from a cloth ball stuffed with feathers thrown by the bowler. In the early form the defenders used their hands, but later a paddle became standard equipment.

There are several references to stoolball in seventeenth-century literature, as well as evidence of its being played in Lancashire, Yorkshire, and Wales. By the eighteenth century, ways of playing the game had varied. Dr. Johnson describes the game in his dictionary of 1755 as "a play where balls are driven from stool to

stool," one of several references that suggest the game was confused with early forms of other sports such as golf. In the 1840s,
the game saw a resurgence in popularity among the local Sussex women; intervillage matches were arranged, and a modern
set of rules was eventually codified in 1841. Stoolball maintained
a reputation as a female sport until the 1920s, when Major William W. Grantham seized upon it and its long history as a sport to
entertain wounded soldiers from World War I and to patriotically
celebrate the British national identity. In parts of Sussex, the game
is still played today, with refined rules and specially made paddles,
though the traditional uniform of the thick and itchy farmer's
smock was left to die a quiet death.

STOOL-BALL.

THE *Ball* once ftruck with Art and
        Care,
And drove impetuous through the Air
Swift round his Courfe the *Gamefter*
        flies,
Or his *Stool's* taken by Surprize.

Stool-ball, as depicted in *A Little Pretty Pocket-Book, intended for the
Amusement of Little Master Tommy and Pretty Miss Polly with Two
Letters from Jack the Giant Killer* by John Newbery (1744).

TIP-CAT

Tip-cat, also called cat and dog, one-a-cat, and piggy, is a game that dates back to the seventeenth century, and was a common sight up until the early twentieth century. There were many versions, because the rules were often improvised. A basic description doesn't quite do justice to the amount of fun that was had, because that description is: the player hits a small stick with a larger stick. A distant grandparent to modern bat-and-ball games, tip-catters used a club (referred to as a dog) about three feet long to bat the cat, a four-inch long wooden stick tapered at the ends. The cat was set up on the ground inside a drawn circle, which the player would then strike to send it spinning away as far as possible. One version involved bases for the player to round while a fielder retrieved the cat and returned it to home base, an early precursor to games like rounders and baseball; a similar "three strikes" rule was also observed. The points system was based on how far the cat was hit, measured by paces or hops.

Another mode of play is described in Jamieson's dictionary of 1808:

> This is a game for three players at least, who are furnished with clubs. They cut out two holes [in the ground] each about a foot in diameter, seven inches in depth, and twenty-six feet apart; one man guards each hole with his club . . . a cat is pitched by a third person from one hole towards the player at the other, who is to prevent the cat from getting into the hole. If it pitches in the hole, the party who threw it takes his turn with the club. If the cat be struck, the club bearers change places.

Street gangs of children caused havoc in London playing tipcat. In 1853, *Punch* magazine remarked, "This mania for playing at cat is no less absurd than it is dangerous, for it is a game at which nobody seems to win, and which, apparently, has no other aim than the windows of the houses and the heads of the passersby."

TORTOISE RACING

I n April 1938, the *Times* received a letter from a furious Methodist minister condemning a local sport that he feared could develop into a national popularism. The Reverend Ralph F. Allport of Weymouth claimed to have witnessed instances of men racing tortoises in the public houses of south Dorset, and was outraged that the game—in which tortoises with tiny plastic jockeys strapped to their shells inched across the cloth of a billiards table toward a pile of lettuce leaves—was permitted to take place. "How would the people who watch them crawl across a billiards table amid ribald laughter and jeers like to be similarly treated?" he thundered, apparently unfamiliar with the standard Friday night goings-on in the average British pub. Cyril Frampton, one of the originators of the pub sport, rejected the idea that it was an unsavory activity. "It's all harmless fun," he told journalists, "entirely free from cruelty. We do not allow betting."

The owner of one of the local Weymouth champions, a small tortoise called Herbert, shared the secret of how to train a champion: "My boy aged five sings to him," he said. " 'Sing Me to Sleep' seems to move Herbert considerably." The owner of Tishy, meanwhile, who had recently come second to Herbert in a nail-biting neck-and-necker, revealed that she trained the reptile by dragging a piece of jam-smeared bread ahead of it on a string. Popeye's success, on the other hand, was attributed to his strict diet of lilies-of-the-valley.

Though the outbreak of World War II put a stop to the practice in Britain, for the British soldiers stationed in Greece on the foothills of Mount Olympus the sport was the sole source of entertainment. The *New Scientist* columnist Patrick Ryan recalled his time as a "leading Greek tortoise impresario," organizing races by tempting the tortoises with shade and fresh lettuce. With plenty of time to kill, the men experimented with different training techniques. "All electric aids were banned, however, after the fourth race," Ryan recalled, "when a nomadic racer went off course, nudged the sergeant major's ankles, and drew blue sparks from the tag-ends of his bootlaces."

Surprisingly, turtle racing could be quite dangerous—but only for those who tried to kiss the turtle. (*Corbis*)

In America, turtle racing had enjoyed newspaper headlines since 1902, when the *Chicago Daily Tribune* reported a race between seven giant turtles ridden by children, dubbing it "The Strangest Race Ever Run." In 1911 the sport was given the celebrity seal of approval by the playwright George Ade and former Massachusetts governor Ebenezer Sumner Draper, who raced turtles while on a Caribbean cruise.

Though a charming sight, the sport was not without its dangers, due to the temperament of the animals. In 1979 a race between a group of American turtles was brought to a temporary standstill when a female spectator bent down to plant a kiss on one of the contestants and it bit down on her lip. The poor woman was released only after paramedics injected the turtle with valium.

TUHO

Tuho, or "pitch-pot" (also Mandarin Chinese *touhu*, Japanese *tōko*), is a traditional game with an ancient history in both China and Korea, to where it later spread. The goal was to throw arrows into a vase from a distance. The earliest mentions of the sport are found in the *Commentary of Zuo* (左傳), written sometime before 389 BC, which describes a game of tuho played by a group of noblemen in 530 BC, as does the *Records of the Grand Historian* (first century BC). Amazingly, physical remains of some of the earliest ceramic pitch pots also survive, such as those from the Western Han Dynasty (206 BC–AD 9) that were discovered in 1969 in the eastern Chinese city of Jiyuan.

The basic gameplay was relatively simple, but the extensive

decorum and ceremony that had to be observed during a match was complex. Among the *Sacred Books of the East*, a gargantuan fifty-volume set of English translations of significant Asian texts published between 1879 and 1910, is a translation of the rules of tuho, which shows there was a complicated procedure to beginning the game:

> The host entreats one of the guests, saying, "I have here these crooked arrows, and this pot with its wry mouth; but we beg you to amuse yourself with them." The guest says, "I have partaken, Sir, of your excellent drink and admirable viands; allow me to decline this further proposal for my pleasure." The host rejoins, "It is not worth the while for you to decline these poor arrows and pot; let me earnestly beg you to try them." The guest repeats his refusal, saying, "I have partaken (of your entertainment), and you would still further have me enjoy myself; I venture firmly to decline." The host again addresses his request in the same words, and then the guest says, "I have firmly declined what you request, but you will not allow me to refuse; I venture respectfully to obey you."

The host would then spin around, saying, "Let me get out of the way," and the game began. The players would take their places ten paces or so from their respective pots, where they were presented with four arrows, which varied in length from eighteen to twenty-eight centimeters. They then had to score a direct hit into the pot, which was filled with beans to prevent the arrows from bouncing out. For each point scored the contestant placed a marker by his foot, the ground acting as a scoreboard for all to see.

Tuho was brought to Korea by visiting Chinese and became instantly popular; the earliest evidence of tuho being played on the peninsula dates to 37 BC–AD 668, where it was played by both men and women and found fans in royalty such as Prince Yangnyong (1394–1462) and King Hyeonjong of Joseon (1641–1674).

One major contributing reason to its success was the fact that tuho was also commonly played as a drinking game. Every time his arrow missed the pot, the loser (*bulseung*, failure) would kneel and take a drink of wine. The winners (*hyeon*, wise) would helpfully top up their cups. Anyone refusing to drink had another option: they were allowed to sing a song as a penalty instead.

UNIVERSAL FOOTBALL

It was the winter of 1933 in Australia. The English cricket team had recently toured and beaten their hosts in the five-Test Ashes series 4–1. The Pommies were led by Douglas Jardine, who had cemented his hated status among the Australian crowds by introducing the aggressive body line, or fast-leg theory. This was an unsporting but legal tactic of short-pitched bowling that sent the ball bouncing high into the batsman's body on the side of the leg stump, often forcing deflections caught by fieldsmen waiting in position close by. The tour had stirred up a high volume of ill feeling between the two nations, and defeat in their cherished sport had left a dent in Australian national pride. It was this sore sentiment that inspired one man to conceive of a sport that was uniquely Australian, which, if successful, could spread across the world, glorifying its country of origin. The man's name was Horrie Miller, secretary of the New South Wales Rugby Football League (NSWRFL), and the plan was to fuse together the two sports of Australian Rules football and rugby into one formidable game to be called "universal football."

Miller had discussed the idea with Con Hickey, secretary of both the Australian National Football Council (ANFC) and the Victorian Football League (VFL), and the pair decided to compose a rule book that would take the best aspects of each sport while maintaining a focus on enjoyability for players and spectators. On its announcement, the idea of crossbreeding the two sports to produce something new with a hybrid vigor caused excitement in the sporting world. "Just imagine it," said James Joynton Smith, patron of the NSWRFL, "the game featuring that outstanding high-marking and cultivated drop-kicking of the Australian Rules, and those brilliant passing movements, sizzling wing runs, and the side-stepping and dodging of rugby."

Miller laid out the rules: players on each side would play on an oval-shaped pitch; tries carried three points, goals two. Rugby tackles were kept, but scrums were replaced with the referee bouncing the ball off the ground. The knock-on and forward-pass rules of rugby were also retained, but bouncing the ball mid-run and airborne tackling were forbidden.

Miller was hopeful for the sport, and a demonstration match was organized to coincide with the Sydney Australian Rules Carnival as an experiment; however, his great rival Harold "Jersey" Flegg, the chairman of the NSWRFL, was against the idea, accusing Miller of being disloyal to the sport. Others pointed out that the issue of offside had not been addressed, a concern Miller dismissed with the reassurance that the NSWRFL "possess a certain amount of administrative and inventive genius."

Preparations went ahead, and the first-ever game of universal football was held on Friday, August 11, at Sydney's agricultural grounds. It was also to be the last. By this point the game had been further modified: the teams were now made up of fourteen men, and the division of regulations essentially meant that the two center quarters of the pitch were subject to football rules, while play in the quarters at each end operated under rugby regulations. The players enlisted for the experiment were so confused that they reportedly carried a copy of the rules around with them during the game. The match was a mess, and dragged on interminably. Not long afterwards, the NSWRFL's general committee voted overwhelmingly in favor of abandoning the idea. Miller was forced to concede failure, and the sport was never spoken of again.

VENATIO

All that with potent Teeth command the Plain,
All that run horrid with erected Mane,
Or proud of stately Horns, or bristling Hair,
At once the Forest's Ornament and Fear;
Torn from their Deserts by the Roman Power,
Nor Strength can save, nor craggy Dens secure.
Claudian (ca. AD 370–404)

As the Roman Empire expanded and formed new provinces in increasingly far-flung lands, prizes of discovery were sent home for exhibition to a public fascinated by the novelties of alien territory—the most popular of which were wild animals. Strange beasts such as lions, elephants, bears, ostriches, goats, deer, and wild dogs were all brought home to Rome for inclusion in the *venationes*. These were one of several grand public *ludi* (games) staged in the circuses of the city, which also included chariot races, athletics, drama, gladiatorial combat, and the previously examined *naumachiae*. The public appetite for such events was insatiable. The games were used to celebrate military triumphs and special occasions, but politicians also found their own popularity could be greatly magnified by staging their own *ludi*.

Initially, the animals were simply put on show as strange sights for the people to gawk at, such as the 142 elephants brought over from Sicily in 251 BC by Lucius Metellus, but this failed to live up

An arena fight between an auroch, a bear, wolves, and a lion, as imagined by Stradanus.

to the excitement of the bloodier games, and so the *venatio* was devised, the first taking place in 186 BC. In *venatio*, the creatures were pitted both against each other and against men in staged arena hunts dedicated to Diana, the goddess of beasts and hunting, and public sacrifice. No expense was spared to bring the most exotic of creatures together in battle, and importing the stock became big business. The species of animals matched was kept varied to maintain public interest: one might see a lion fight a bull one day, and a rhinoceros charge an Atlas bear the next. Sometimes a fair fight was passed up in favor of an altogether bloodier spectacle, like a pack of dogs being released into the arena to tear apart a single deer. There are even references suggesting land predators were set against sea creatures when the amphitheaters were flooded for aquatic games like the mock sea battles:

Nor Sylvan Monsters we alone have view'd,
But huge Sea-Calves, dy'd red with hostile Blood
Of Bears, lie flound'ring in the wond'rous Flood.
(Calpurnius, Eclogue 7)

As one might expect, the death tolls at such events were catastrophic. One *venatio* staged at the Circus Maximus in 169 BC saw the deaths of 63 leopards, 40 bears, and several elephants. In 55 BC, 500 lions, 410 panthers and leopards, and 18 elephants were slaughtered in five days. A *venatio* thrown by Julius Caesar saw 400 lions destroyed in one event, while in another of his events 500 footmen were pitched against 20 elephants, with 20 more carrying manned turrets on their backs. Some 500 bears were executed in one day at the order of Caligula to honor Drusilla;

9,000 animals were killed in the inaugural games of the Colosseum; while upon the return of Trajan from Dacia, an assortment of 11,000 animals was sacrificed.

There were two groups of men who were sent into the arena to battle the animals: the *bestiarii* and the *venatores*. The latter were trained, professional hunters; but the *bestiarii* (beast fighters) were usually a wretched bunch made up of condemned criminals and prisoners of war. Underequipped and with no training, their role was to provide a gruesome spectacle for the crowd by dying helplessly. This was often staged in a theatrical manner, with the unarmed *bestiarius* introduced to the crowd as one character and an enraged bear as another. Cicero writes of one lion sent in to dispatch two hundred men. Theirs was a hopeless position, and they knew it. The stoic philosopher Seneca (ca. BC–AD 65) commends the bravery of a German prisoner who chose to ram a lavatory sponge down his own throat and asphyxiate rather than face the death that awaited him in the arena, while another threw himself headfirst into the wheel of a moving cart to break his own neck. Symmachus (ca. 345–402) writes of twenty-nine Saxon captives who strangled each other the night before they were due to tread the circus sand. With such stories of despair it is astonishing, then, that some *bestiarii* fought by choice, for a small salary, though enjoyed better training at schools similar to those established for the instruction of gladiators.

The spectators were protected from the animals by ditches and raised platforms, but in a cunning move to win the crowd, Gordian I introduced a new form of *venatio* in which the public were able to participate. For the *venatio direptionis*, a specially built "forest" was erected in the center of the circus with transplanted trees, and hundreds of animals such as boar, sheep, ostriches, and deer were released into the arena. The public was invited to enter the enclosure and attempt to catch the game, with permission to keep whatever they managed to kill. Often *tesserae* (tickets) were scattered among the participants with instructions to chase a particular animal, with prize money offered to the first person able to seize their designated prey.

VIKING SPORTS

It should come as no surprise that the ways in which the Vikings chose to relax were almost as violent as the bloody raids and pillages for which the seaborne Scandinavians are renowned. At home, most were farmers and fishermen; but when the warmth of summer came and the lure of foreign bounty called, they were warriors of unparalleled ferocity and martial skill. This was partly down to the sports they practiced, which served as military training in the intervening months.

The Vikings were not a literate people, so very few clues about their day-to-day lives exist. They relied instead upon oral tradition and the inscribing of basic runes at significant locations. In fact, most of our understanding of the marauders comes from sources written centuries later, such as the enthralling Icelandic sagas, and other information passed on from generations of storytelling. Fortunately for our purposes, several mentions are made in these histories of their sporting pastimes, and when combined with archaeological evidence we gain glimpses of how these games, or *leikar*, were played. Gatherings for sporting events (*leikmot*) were grand social occasions, and both men and women came together in celebration (though it appears that only the men took part in most of the sports). Forms of hunting and basic feats of strength such as lifting boulders were common, but the following are a few of the lesser-known (and more bizarre) of these events.

Bone-throwing (*hnútukast*)

Sometimes elaborate rules and imaginative gameplay just get in the way of a good braining. In this sport, the men hurled bones at each other, with intent to cause injury. *Hnútukast* is mentioned in the *Bárðar saga Snæfellsáss*, one of the later *Íslendingasaga* with fantastical elements, dated to the fourteenth century. In the second section, Bárðar's son, Gestr, saves his half brother Þórðr from a *þurs* (giant) named Kolbjörn after the two play a match. Following a raucous meal in a cave full of men and monsters, Kolbjörn asks what they should do to amuse themselves, proposing *glíma* (see below) or *hnútukast*. To answer his question, a character named Glámur takes a large bone from his plate and flings it at Þórðr. Gestr catches it in midair and hurls it back at Glámur with such force that the man's eye is knocked from his head to dangle against his face. This is taken a step further in *Hrólfs saga kraka*, when Böðvarr returns a bone so hard that it strikes a man dead.

Drowning (*sund*)

In its Viking definition, the sport of "swimming" consisted of two competitors wrestling with each other underwater to prevent the other from surfacing and catching his breath. In *The Saga of the People of Laxárdalr* (thirteenth century), Kjartan Ólafsson and his men go to "swim" in the River Nid, now known as the Nidelva. There they encounter a local townsman who was known as "the best of the sport." (This man later turns out to be King Olaf Trygvason.) Kjartan decides to challenge him. He jumps into the river, swims over to the man, "and drags him forthwith under and keeps him down for awhile, and then lets him go up again. And when they had been up for a long while, this man suddenly clutches Kjartan and drags him under; and they keep down for such a time as Kjartan thought quite long enough, when up they come a second time." Throughout the match, the men never said a word to each other. In the final and longest round, as the men grappled to keep each other beneath the water, "Kjartan now mis-doubted him how this play would end, and thought he had never before found himself in such a tight place; but at last they come up and strike out for the bank. Then said the townsman, 'Who is this man?' Kjartan told him his name. The townsman said, 'You are very deft at swimming.' "

Glíma

Glíma is a Viking martial art first mentioned by the poet Bragi Boddason (790–850), who tells the story of the Norse god Thor traveling to Útgarða-Loki. Thor, who among his many roles was also worshipped as the god of wrestling, drunkenly challenges any of the men in the hall to a fight. The story is also recounted in the *Prose Edda* (thirteenth century), which relates that Útgarða-Loki responds to Thor's challenge by suggesting he fight his elderly nurse, Elli, a frail woman "stricken with years." Unknown to Thor, Elli is the spirit of old age. "That struggle went in such wise that the harder Thor strove in gripping, the faster she stood; then the old woman essayed a hold, and then Thor became totty on his feet, and their tuggings were very hard. Yet it was not long before Thor fell to his knee, on one foot."

The fighting system of throws, holds, and blows was employed to devastating effect by the Norsemen. During a glíma in *Gunnars saga Keldugnúpsfifls*, Gunnar lifts his adversary into the air and slams him down onto a bench, breaking his back. To counter the risk of broken bones, some wore a protective padded jacket called a *fangastakkur*. In *Kjalnesinga Saga*, Búi is saved by his *fangastakkur* when he is thrown against a *fanghella* (a flat standing stone commonly positioned in designated *glíma* fields into which one could smash the limbs and spine of one's opponent). With the protection of his *fangastakkur*, Búi deflects the blow and instead throws his enemy against the stone. He then jumps onto his back, shattering the man's ribs and killing him instantly. In a later chapter of his saga, the aforementioned Gunnar uses the stone in a similar manner to cleave a man in two.

Horse fighting (*hestavíg*)

Horse fights were baitings in which two loose stallions were encouraged to battle over a mare in heat tethered nearby. The fight was brought to an end only when one of the animals fled or, more commonly, was killed by the other. As it is understood, the match was cheered on by a surrounding crowd who gambled on the outcome, the horse owners intervening with a wooden staff when needed. In *Reykdæla saga ok Víga-Skútu*, Eyjólf's horse bites down on Bjarni's stallion and has to be prized off with the stick. The men would also grab hold of a horse's tail to drive their fighter into a fury, while another tactic was to push the horse forward. The latter came with its own danger, as discovered by Þorgeir and Kolur in *Brennu-Njáls saga* when Gunnar pushes in return, and the horse falls back onto the men and crushes them. The practice lasted as a folk tradition long after the Viking era passed, with the bishop of Oslo describing the game in 1618:

> About a mile and a half from Fyresdal a crowd of people con-gregates on St. Bartholomew's Day with their horses from the districts all round, and the horses are left to bite each other two by two, the notion being that when they bite each other two by two, there will be a good crop and vice versa.

Knattleikr

The rules of how to play the popular *knattleikr* (ball game) have long since been forgotten, as have the details of the field on which it was played, but from descriptions the game appears to most closely resemble Irish hurling. In *Grettis saga*, which follows the violent exploits of the pugnacious outlaw Grettir the Strong, it's mentioned that a game of *knattleikr* was played at Miðfjarðarvatn in Iceland, an annual autumnal venue for the sport. Two teams lined up against each other, each man matched against an opponent of equal size. The game lasted for the entire day, and violence was encouraged. The players competed with bats, but were also allowed to catch the ball and run with it while being chased by the opposition. One thing is certain: while the game itself was a brutal affair, the real action happened when arguments during matches turned into brawls. The modestly statured Grettir, for example, was humiliated when Auðun hit the ball over his head, so he retrieved it and threw it at Auðun, hitting him between the eyes and drawing blood. Auðun swung at Grettir with his bat, and the two men fought on the ground, eventually having to be separated by their teammates. The most striking escalation of temper, though, is displayed by Egil Skallagrímsson in *Egil's Saga*. In return for being manhandled earlier in the match, Egil chases after the player, tackles him, and splits his skull with an axe. What is particularly impressive about this is that at the time Egil was six years old.

Scraper game (*sköfuleikr*)

In *The Legendary Saga of St. Olaf*, it's mentioned that Olaf's absent father had been killed during a *leíkmot*, specifically during a *sköfuleikr*, or scraper game. Again we are short on details, but it seems to have been a violent combat involving the use of pot scrapers made from cow horn. The players were frequently intoxicated on both ale (not unique to the scraper game) and a hallucinogenic tea brewed from powdered mushrooms. Just as with *knattleikr*, the game lasted all day and could end with a body count: during one game described in *Harðar saga og Hólmverja*, seven people died, a tally that included Önundr, who paused during the journey home from the match to tie his shoe and promptly died from his injuries.

Skin-pulling

Finally, we come to skin-pulling, a Viking variation on the classic game of tug-of-war that is perhaps the least known entertainment of the Norsemen. The main reference for the sport is *Hjalmter and Olver's Saga*, in which Hörd and Hástigi compete in a hall in the early hours of the morning in a match overseen by their king. In preparation, Hástigi stripped naked, but Hörd retained his thick fur coat. They were then presented with a strong walrus hide to serve as the rope and took their places on either side of a fire in the center of the room, with the skin stretched over the flames. The men then began to ferociously tug on the skin, trying to drag the other forward into the fire. This went on for some time, and they were beginning to tire when Hörd said to Hástigi: "Look out; for now I will use my strength, and thou wilt not live long." Hástigi scoffed at this, but "Hörd then pulled with all his strength, and pulled Hástigi forward into the fire, and threw the hide over him; he jumped on his back, and then went to his bench. The king ordered them to take the man out of the fire; he was much burnt."

VINKENSPORT

Finching" is a Flemish sport of medieval origin that to this day has a small, dedicated following in Belgium, parts of the Netherlands, and Germany, despite the continued protestations of animal welfare groups. Also known as finch sport or finch fitting, the competitions see around fifty *vinkeniers*, or finch trainers, sit side by side in a long row, usually along a road, with a wooden box at their feet. Inside each box is a male finch, chosen by the trainer for his singing ability and stamina. A timekeeper waving a large red flag signals the start of the hour-long match, and the spectators, trainers, and judges wait in hushed silence for the action to begin. As the males begin their song, calling out to nearby females and warning other males of their territory, the number of "susk-e-wiets" (as this type of call is referred to) produced by the birds are recorded, and when the hour is up the bird that tweeted the most is announced as the winner.

The rules are strict: the utterance of one wrong note, such as a "susk-e-*wiat*," means instant disqualification, as do instances of

A bird being blinded for vinkensport.

cheating, such as the recent case of the trainer whose bird won several matches in a row with the exact same score of 725 each time. A suspicious judge opened the *vinkenier*'s box and found inside a miniature CD player. Rumors of doping also plagued one champion finch named Schauvlieghe, who won his title with a record-shattering score of 1,278 susk-e-wiets. The allegations that this came about because Schauvlieghe had been driven into a libidinous frenzy through testosterone injections were never conclusively proven.

In fact, needles feature prominently in the dark history of *vinkensport*, for up until the early 1900s *vinkeniers* indulged in a particularly gruesome pre-match preparation: the birds were blinded with hot needles, which was thought to prevent distraction and encourage more frequent singing. The sport was also practiced in this way in pubs around England before World War I. Thomas Hardy, a staunch supporter of the RSPCA, wrote his poem "The Blinded Bird" in protest against the practice, which was finally brought to an end in 1920 following a campaign fronted by a group of blinded war veterans.

WALKING-STICK FIGHTING

On February 21, 1814, a man in full British military uniform entered the Ship Inn in Dover, England. Warming his hands by the fire, he introduced himself as Colonel du Bourg, aide-de-camp to Lord Cathcart, and happily declared to the room that after eleven years of bloody war Napoleon had finally been slain by a group of Cossacks. The drinkers were overjoyed, and the colonel continued his journey to London, stopping at inns along the way to make the same announcement. At midday, as the news was slowly filtering through the countryside, a group of men in French military dress drove a carriage through the center of London distributing leaflets proclaiming the news. There was mass celebration in the streets, and at the London Stock Exchange the price of government bonds and securities soared. However, that afternoon the government announced that Napoleon was very much alive—the city had fallen victim to a masterful hoax. The value of the stock plummeted. The Committee of the London Stock Exchange suspected foul play and launched an investigation, and it was discovered that a huge quantity of government securities had been sold just as the price had reached its zenith. An analysis of who stood to gain was performed, and a group of men including the naval hero Sir Thomas Cochrane was arrested, with heavy fines and prison sentences of one year dished out. The story of what became known as the Great Stock Exchange Fraud of 1814 later influenced the plot of Alexandre Dumas's 1844 novel *The Count of Monte Cristo.*

This story is mentioned here not just to brush the dust off a thrilling piece of history worthy of its own Hollywood depiction but because it is the perfect introduction to the eccentric human firework show that was Captain Charles Random de Berenger, one of those complicit in the fraud. The captain was found guilty of impersonating du Bourg and one of the French officers and was sentenced to twelve months in prison, a £1,000 fine, and an hour in the pillory. For most men this episode would be a profoundly deflating experience, but not for de Berenger. Though he turned from a life of crime, his entrepreneurial spirit was undampened by his stay in the notorious Marshalsea prison. He met and married a wealthy German baroness, and with his newfound wealth he purchased a Chelsea villa with eleven acres of grounds to indulge his passion for athletics. There he built "THE STADIUM, Cremorne House, Chelsea, established for the tuition and practice of skillful and manly exercises generally," an outdoor gymnasium with the motto: "Nothing is difficult for him who has the will." He also produced a book in the same vein, *Helps and Hints: How to Protect Life and Property* (1835). Though dismissed by one reviewer as "a clap-trap of gymnastics," the self-protection handbook was a hit and became a key text in the art of employing the walking stick as an instrument of self-defense (as well as offering guidance on how to escape from freezing waters, burning buildings, highwaymen,

Charles Random de Berenger's *Helps and Hints: How to Protect Life and Property* (1835) shows how to put a walking stick to excellent use.

street ruffians, and enraged bulls). Berenger focuses predominantly on training his reader to dissuade potential muggers from selecting them as targets: "To be courageous is enviable, whilst, on the other hand, to be able to conceal the absence of courage is useful." Aided by some terrific illustrations he then explores the various maneuvers and "cuts" one should make with the stick, including when one comes under gang attack, with prose so energetic one can imagine the baron waving a walking stick in one hand while writing with the other:

> If hemmed in thus by numbers, *thrust or poke* with *either* end at *any* of your assailants who lay themselves open; always doing it as *forcibly* and as *rapidly* as possible, and chiefly directing such pokes at their *faces* and *stomachs*, hitting occasionally, as opportunity offers, smart blows, which, however, from their contraction of the proper length, will not serve you so well as forcible threats . . . *Kick* the *shins* of such fellows at the same time . . .

Of course, the good baron was not the first to devise the martial art: stick fighting can be found in the sporting histories of cultures across the world. For example, the introduction of bamboo practice swords in the Japanese discipline of kendo dates back to the Shōtoku era (1711–1716), while in Ireland fighting with the shillelagh was employed as a form of judicial combat akin to dueling with pistols and was incorporated into the Irish stick fighting martial art *bataireacht*. The bulb-headed walking stick is produced from the resilient root of the blackthorn tree and is given its customary toughness and glossy surface by smearing it with lard and hanging it to cure in a chimney for a few days. The shillelagh is a form of cudgel, a weapon that also has a long history in England. Cudgeling (fighting with two sticks), together with singlestick, was a form of fencing with canes and clubs that emerged primarily as a safe way to practice sword fighting; although, as has been demonstrated numerous times in this book, the definition of "safe" has varied wildly over the years. Essentially, it was clubbing about the head. Cudgeling's popularity bloomed in the eighteenth century, when matches were played before large crowds at fairs and even at horse racing meets such as Ascot. Points were scored by "breaking head," i.e., drawing blood—"No Head to be deemed broke unless the Blood runs an Inch," declared an advertisement in *Jackson's Oxford Journal* for a match in 1753.

On the details of singlestick, the best illumination is given by a penman for William Hone's *Year-Book* (1829), who wrote:

> The single-stick player having the left hand tied down, and using only one stick both to defend himself and strike his antagonist. The object of each gamester in this play, as in cudgelling, is to guard himself, and to fetch blood from the other's head; whether by taking a little skin from his pericranium, or drawing a stream from his nose, or knocking out a few . . . teeth.

The inexpensive sport became a favorite of the people and was played en masse in giant street brawls, usually impromptu but sometimes announced ahead of time, such as that advertised in *Sarah Farley's Bristol Journal* of May 7, 1774:

To be played for at Back Sword [aka singlestick] at Wotton under Edge, on the Tuesday and Wednesday in the Whitsun Week, Twenty guineas, viz. 8 guineas the first day by nine men on each side, and 12 guineas the second day by eleven men on each side. Each couple to play 'till one of their heads is broken. The side which gets the odd head to have the prize. No padding allowed.

WATERFALL-RIDING

Every second, around twenty-eight million liters of water pour down the three waterfalls of Niagara, located between the Canadian province of Ontario and the American state of New York. When tourism began to develop into an industry in eighteenth-century America, Niagara Falls was the destination of choice for the new holidaymakers, who would become the region's main source of revenue. But among the crowds of tourists and honeymooners who flocked to the attraction there walked a different breed of visitor, entirely unconcerned with sightseeing: this was the daredevil.

The most famous of these were the tightrope walkers, or "funambulists," who in the early days of the sport enjoyed a total absence of regulation. The most celebrated of the wiremen was Jean François Gravelet, known as The Great Blondin, who made his first successful crossing along a rope 1,100 feet long at Niagara on June 30, 1859. That summer he made eight further successful walks, hitting the headlines by performing a crossing while carrying his manager, Harry Colcord, on his back. Blondin was a global hero, and his fame inspired a host of other tightrope walkers, such as Samuel Dixon, Clifford Calverly, Henry Bellini, and Stephen Peer, to attempt the crossing. Peer's story is a particularly interesting one. In 1873 he was working as an assistant to Bellini, and helped set up the equipment with which his employer would make his crossing. However, perhaps drunk on the spirit of adventure, Peer decided to give the stunt a go himself, and when his master turned his back he strode out onto the wire to the cheers of onlookers. Bellini was so outraged by the limelight theft that he started to sever the tightrope. Several bystanders wrestled the homicidal funambulist to the ground, and Peer was able to complete the walk, eventually going on to a greater level of fame than his former employer. He made his last crossing on June 22, 1887; three days later his body was found on the bank of the Niagara River, below his rope. The intoxicating spirit of adventure replaced with intoxicating spirits, Peer had attempted to walk the rope again after a night of heavy drinking, and had fallen in his first few steps.

Meanwhile, at the base of the falls, aquatic daredevilry was in full swing. Men leapt into the whirlpools of the Niagara River to cross the waters and collect generous prizes. Captain Matthew Webb, a professional English swimmer who in 1875 had daubed himself in porpoise oil to become the first person to swim the English Channel, confidently dived into the rapids in 1883, despite failing to find sponsorship for the venture amid warnings that it was an act of suicide. His body was found four days later, downriver in Lewiston, New York. Robert Watson later wrote of his friend: "His object was not suicide, but money, and imperishable fame." As well as the swimmers, there were the barrel riders:

Carlisle Graham was an English cooper who became the first person to seal himself up in the container and survive being thrown into the great white waters in 1886. He immediately announced his desire to improve on the feat and, in 1887, again rode a barrel down the rapids, this time with his head protruding, unprotected. Miraculously he prevailed, though he was left profoundly deaf. Undeterred, in 1901 he enlisted his friend Maude Willard to participate in a joint effort—she would ride the barrel to the whirlpool, and then the both of them would swim to Lewiston. Unfortunately, Maude decided to take a passenger in the barrel— her pet fox terrier. As they began their journey the dog panicked in the tiny space and rammed its muzzle into the airhole in a desperate bid for freedom. The barrel bounced around in the whirlpool for several hours before rescuers were able to get to it, by which time poor Maude had suffocated.

As the nineteenth century drew to a close, the number of barrel riders was steadily increasing, yet still no one had dared attempt the ultimate barrel stunt: to plummet over the edge of the Falls. This was reckoned by every man in the game to be certain self-destruction, and so it took a woman to prove them wrong. In 1901, a schoolmistress named Annie Edson Taylor decided she would take the plunge on October 24, her sixty-third birthday. Taylor was convinced that the barrel ride over Horseshoe Falls (a drop of some 150 feet) would garner her enough money to avoid retirement to the poorhouse; and so, with the help of a manager named Frank M. Russell, she set up the event, advertising herself as the "Heroine of Niagara Falls." A custom-made four-and-a-half-foot barrel was constructed. Inside were straps, a mattress for cushioning, and an iron anvil in the base for balance.

Some people celebrate their sixty-third birthday quietly,
but Annie Edson Taylor decided to jump Niagara Falls
in a barrel—though not before testing it out
on her cat first. (*Bridgeman*)

After an airhole was drilled in the side it was determined that the vessel should undergo a trial run with a live passenger. There was little chance of finding a volunteer, however, and so the honor went to Taylor's pet cat, Iagara. The tabby survived the journey, badly shaken but physically unscathed, and so Taylor decided to proceed.

Clutching her lucky heart-shaped pillow, she was sealed into the barrel with screws and a bicycle pump to pressurize the compartment and placed in a small rowboat. Barrel and rider were then taken out and dumped with a splash into the Niagara River, just north of Little Grass Island on the New York State side. The barrel bobbed upright as it drifted to the precipice, and then plummeted to the waters below. Thirty minutes later her team managed to reach the barrel and drag it to shore. The lid was unscrewed and Taylor was found to be in shock but alive, with only minimal bruising and cuts. Upon emerging, her first words were, "I prayed every second, except when I went unconscious." After her cuts were attended to and she'd been handed a stiff drink, she was asked by a member of the press what the experience had been like. She responded: "If it was with my dying breath, I would caution anyone against attempting the feat . . . I would sooner walk up to the mouth of a cannon, knowing it was going to blow me to pieces, than make another trip over the Fall."

In the end, Taylor made very little money from her record-setting barrel ride. Her manager, Russell, ran off with her barrel, and she spent a considerable portion of her earnings hiring private detectives trying to find it. She spent the rest of her years running her own souvenir stand, posing for photographs and offering psychic services.

Several others attempted to follow in her wake, with varying success. An Englishman named Bobby Leach survived the fall in 1911, though he spent twenty-three weeks recovering in hospital. (Having fully recuperated, he would later die after slipping on an orange peel while on a lecture tour in New Zealand.) Another Englishman, Charles Stephens, tried the stunt on July 11, 1920. Upon impact his body shot straight through the bottom of his barrel; only his arm was recovered. Altogether, in the years since Annie Taylor first showed it to be possible, fifteen people have successfully survived sailing over the waterfalls in a craft, while five have been less fortunate.

WOLFING

Perhaps the best demonstration of the intensity with which wolves were feared and hated was their legal synonymity with the murderer. In early medieval England, when a killer fled justice for the safety of the forest, a "Writ of Outlawry" was announced that declared *Caput gerat lupinum*, "Let his be a wolf's head," rendering that person as low as a wolf in the eyes of the law (indeed, "wolf's head" was a popular alternative term for "outlaw"). This meant that, just as with wolves, anyone was legally permitted to kill him on sight.

There was reason behind this detestation: wolves terrorized. They ravaged flocks, decimated herds, and attacked humans. They killed so much cattle in Sutherland in 1577 that James VI ordered it be compulsory to hunt wolves three times a year. Across Scotland, the creatures posed such a serious threat to journeyers that special shelters called spittals were built along the roads to offer protection in the event of attack. Not even the dead were safe: the desecration of burial sites by wolves was a constant problem. Wolves exhumed and fed upon the deceased inhabitants of Eddrachillis so often that the townspeople resorted to ferrying their dead for burial to the island of Handa, off the west coast of Scotland. The islands of Tanera Mòr and Inishail were also used as alternative burial sites, while in the earldom of Atholl the people were driven to building coffins with flagstones to keep their tenants safe from gnawing. Battlefields were veritable Jacobean feasts: Gerald of Wales wrote how the wolves of Holywell came out en masse to feast on the corpses left over from Henry II's bloody incursion into Wales in 1165.

While technically a year-round activity, wolf hunting was most popular in the first three months of the year, for the animals found it harder to detect traps in the seasonal weather. Unlike the hunts of other species, which involved various restrictions, the challenge of wolf killing was opened to all. Indeed, it was heartily encouraged: King John offered as much as ten shillings for the head and pelts of a wolf pair. When lands were granted, a common condition was that the title should include the obligation to perform the public service of wolf extirpation, or "to hunt whensoever the king should command." William de Limeres, for example, was bestowed lands at Comelessend in Hampshire "by the service of hunting the Wolf with the king's dogs." Under Edward III's rule, Thomas Engaine enjoyed lands in Pytchley in Northampton on the proviso that he hunt the wolf to extinction in Northampton,

Mastiffs with their spiked collars for wolf hunting, from *The Master of Game* (1413) by Edward of Norwich, the oldest English book on hunting.

Rutland, Oxford, Essex, and Buckingham. In the eleventh year of Henry VI's reign (1433), Sir Robert Plumpton maintained ownership of an estate named "Wolf hunt land" in Nottingham by chasing wolves through Sherwood Forest with dogs and horns. In Scotland, this duty was codified in national legislation:

> . . . *ilk baron within his barony in gangand time*
> *of the year sall chase and seek the quhelpes*
> *of Wolves and gar slay them. And the baron*
> *sall give to the man that slays the Woolfe in*
> *his barony and brings the baron the head,*
> *twa shillings. And when the baron ordains*
> *to hunt and chase the Woolfe, the tenants*
> *sall rise with the baron. And that the barons*
> *hunt in their baronies and chase the Woolfes*
> *four times a year, and als oft as onie Woolfe*
> *beis seen within the barony . . .*

Under Henry I, wolf huntsmen were distinguished by a higher budget of twenty pence a day for horses, men, and dogs (usually numbering twenty-four), something that in the reigns of Henry II, Richard I, and John became a standard annual payment. Traps such as snares and *hausse-pieds* (a noose that when stepped into swung the prey high into the air) and "venomous powders" were the most commonly used equipment, while the breeds of dogs favored for the hunt were the Irish wolfhound and the mighty English mastiff. All were fitted with spiked metal collars, which have survived to this day as a purely aesthetic accessory but back then served a vital purpose. The wolf's natural instinct was to attack the throat of the dog, but with the protection of the collar the dog gained an advantage. Mastiffs were the English dog of choice, mainly due to the fact that the Irish hound was so scarce in the country. In 1156, Conan, Duke of Brittany and Earl of Richmond, visited Jervaulx Abbey in Yorkshire and was so horrified by the abundant wolf population of the area that he gave the monks special dispensation to keep mastiffs for their protection. John le Wolfhonte was also fond of using the breed to hunt down a wolf's lair and destroy its young. In the hunt, the dogs were usually employed to ambush the wolf, which was lured into a clearing with a bloody horse carcass, rather than to hunt *par force* (chase), for as George Turberville wrote in *The Noble Art of Venerie* (1575):

> A Wolfe will stand up a whole day before a good kennel of houndes unless ye Greyhoundes course him . . . I have seen a Wolfe . . . out runne four or five brace of the best Greyhoundes that might be founde.

In England, the last official record of wild wolf existence dates to around 1396, when the monks of Whitby paid ten shillings ninepence for "tawing 14 wolf skins." By the fifteenth century, the wolf in England was extinct. In Scotland, though, it was a different story. In 1563 the Earl of Atholl arranged a wolf drive of epic proportions for Mary, Queen of Scots. It featured 2,000 Scottish beaters, which resulted in a tally of 360 dead deer and five wolves. The animals continued to live under bounty well into the seventeenth century, when (officially) the last wolf of Scotland was killed by Sir Ewan Cameron in 1680 in Killiecrankie, Perthshire.

ACKNOWLEDGMENTS

M y thanks to Charlie Campbell, Ian Marshall, and the team at Simon & Schuster, all the B-Hs, Harry Man, Alex Anstey, Daisy Laramy-Binks, Matthew and Gemma Troughton, Richard Jones, Marie-Eve Poget, Patrick Fischer, Holly Webb, Bruno Cavallaro, Katherine Anstey and Will Walker, Alex Popoff, Kate Awad, Thomas Hodgkinson, Lindsey Fitz-Harris, Clare Spencer, Hope Brimelow, and the staff of the British Library. I am especially grateful to Roger Griffiths and Richard Fattorini at Sotheby's for their invaluable help with sourcing some of the images.

SELECT BIBLIOGRAPHY

Allen, D. (2010) *Otter*. London: Reaktion Books.

Armitage, J. (1977) *Man at Play*. London: Frederick Warne & Co Ltd.

Aspin, J. (1825) *A Picture of the Manners, Customs, Sports, and Pastimes of the Inhabitants of England*. London: J. Harris.

Baillie-Glohman, W. (1913) *Sport in Art*. London: Ballantyne Press.

Bale, J., Cheska, A., Chick, G., Christensen, K., Guttman, A., Holt, R., . . . Park, R. (eds.). (2012) *Encyclopedia of World Sport from Ancient Times to the Present*. Great Barrington: Berkshire, USA.

Blackmore, H. (1971) *Hunting Weapons*. New York: Walker & Company.

Blaine, D. (1879) *An Encyclopedia of Rural Sports*. London: Longmans, Greene, Reader and Dyer.

Bondeson, J. (2011) *Amazing Dogs*. Stroud: Amberley.

Bottomley, J. F. (1869) *The Velocipede, Its Past, Its Present, & Its Future*. London: Simpkin, Marshall.

Braudel, F. (1981) *Civilization and Capitalism 15th–18th Century Vol. 1. The Structures of Everyday Life*. Oakland: University of California Press.

Brunner, B. (2007) *Bears: A Brief History.* New Haven: Yale University Press.

Collins, T., Martin, J., and Vamplew, W. (eds.) (2005) *Encyclopedia of Traditional British Rural Sports.* London: Routledge.

Donaldson, W. (2002) *Rogues, Villains and Eccentrics.* London: Phoenix.

Endrei, W. and Zolnay, L. (1986) *Fun and Games in Old Europe.* Budapest: Corvina.

Fleig, D. (1996) *History of Fighting Dogs.* Neptune City: T. F. H.

Gipe, G. (1978) *The Great American Sports Book.* New York: Dolphin.

Grose, F. (1785) *A Classical Dictionary of the Vulgar Tongue.* London: S. Hooper.

MacGregor, A. (2012) *Animal Encounters.* London: Reaktion Books.

Malcolmson, R. W. (1973) *Popular Recreations in English Society 1700–1850.* Cambridge: Cambridge University Press.

Monelle, R. (2006) *The Musical Topic: Hunt, Military and Pastoral.* Bloomington: Indiana University Press.

Reeves, A. C. (1995) *Pleasures and Pastimes in Medieval England.* Stroud: Sutton.

Strutt, J. (1801) *The Sports and Pastimes of the People of England.* London: Methven & Co.

Stubbes, P. (1583) *The Anatomie of Abuses.* London: Richard Jones.

Turberville, G. (1575) *The Noble Arte of Venerie or Hunting.* London.